Introduction

We have been given an incredible gift in Scripture—the very Word of God, written in ink so that we may know Him. It is life to our souls. Jesus says in Matthew 22:37 that the greatest commandment is to "Love the Lord your God with all your heart, with all your soul, and with all your mind." When we study Scripture, we seek to know and love the God who breathed out its words. When we study Scripture as believers, we not only behold the glory of God in its pages, but we are transformed into His image, "from glory to glory" (2 Corinthians 3:18). When we stand in awe of the immeasurable beauty and power and holiness of God, the Holy Spirit sanctifies us, making us righteous like the God whom we behold. God has graciously revealed Himself specially through His Word, and what a joy it is to seek Him there!

The Word of God is the authority on truth; it tells us who God is, who we are in relation to Him, and how we should live. It is therefore incredibly important to know how to study the Bible well. In this study, it is our hope to help you do just that. In the pages that follow you will find teaching on how to study the Bible, as well as visuals, charts, and workbook pages to help you put it into practice. The study is broken up into weeks and days but is also designed to allow you to work at your own pace. Feel free to complete several workbook pages at once if you feel comfortable with the material, or slow down on a concept that you find more challenging or is unfamiliar to you.

We pray that this study will help equip you to search the Word of God and experience the joy of finding Him there.

give
me

WEEK 4

WEEK 5

WEEK 6

EXTRA RESOURCES

Throughout this study you will find many helpful and practical workbook pages to accompany daily content. In order to get the most out of these resources, we recommend having a few tools readily available for each day:

- [ ] *A Bible with cross references*
- [ ] *Multiple versions of the Bible, or a computer to look up the text in other versions*
- [ ] *Trustworthy commentaries*
- [ ] *A pen & pencil*
- [ ] *A variety of highlighters*
- [ ] *Flags or sticky tabs to mark pages you would like to return to*

First and foremost, the Bible is about God.

Why the Bible is Important

Reading: 2 Peter 1:21, 1 Thessalonians 2:13, 2 Timothy 3:16-17

The Bible is the Word of God. In its pages we discover the character of the One who spoke all things into existence. The Bible contains stories of people throughout time in seasons of joy and sadness, of victory and tragedy, but ultimately, the Bible is not primarily about us. First and foremost, the Bible is about God. To seek to know God is the greatest endeavor we could ever undertake, and it is vitally important that we have a framework by which to approach our study of the Scriptures that reveal Him to us. As we come to God's Word, it is helpful to have an understanding of the nature of the Bible itself. God's Word is inspired, inerrant, sufficient, and eternal.

Scripture is inspired by God. It is not the product of men but of God (I Thessalonians 2:13). It does not just contain truth; it is the truth. 2 Timothy 3:16-17 reveals that all Scripture is given through inspiration; it has been "breathed out" by God. Though God used men to write down the words of Scripture, the words are actually the words of God, and there is no part of the Bible that is not inspired by Him. As the inspired Word of God, the Bible is authoritative as the standard of truth in all areas that it addresses.

Scripture is inerrant, which means that it is without error. Everything recorded in it is accurate. God does not lie, and therefore we can be confident that everything He has recorded in His Word is true (John 17:17, Titus 1:2, Hebrews 6:18). The original manuscripts of Scripture were breathed out by God Himself and without contradictions, discrepancies, or errors of any kind. The inerrancy of Scripture means that God's Word can be trusted because God is completely trustworthy.

Scripture is sufficient. The sufficiency of Scripture means that everything we need to know about God, salvation, and how to live godly lives is found in the Bible. We do not need to look for any further divine revelation because He has already given us everything that we need in His Word. The Word of God points us to the gospel, and it is there that we find all that we need.

Scripture is eternal. It stands the test of time and will never fade away. God has promised that He will preserve His Word, and He has been faithful to that promise (Psalm 12:6-7, Psalm 119:89-91, Matthew 5:18). The Bible is not an outdated book, but it is enduring truth that is just as applicable today as when it was first written.

When we begin to grasp the significance of Scripture and recognize that it is a gift to us, our hearts will desire to open this sacred text and read it. We do not read to simply learn some nice stories or even to solve all of our problems. We come to the Bible to learn who God is and be transformed into His image through the power of His Spirit and the power of the Word of God. The Bible has effective, transformational power in the life of the believer (Isaiah 55:10-11). As we come to this study, we pray that God will transform us into His image through the power of His Word.

Scripture is

INSPIRED BY GOD

INNERANT

SUFFICIENT

ETERNAL

Read 2 Timothy 3:16-17, and record why God's Word is profitable.

How does God's Word equip us for every good work?

If we fully grasped the importance of God's Word, how would our lives change?

Reading: Proverbs 2:1-6, Psalm 119:18

Approaching God's Word Prayerfully

—

We should pray before, during, and after reading God's Word. Praying recognizes our dependency of the Spirit to understand the Word. We can often be quick to jump into our study of Scripture, forgetting that we have no ability to understand it apart from the work of the Holy Spirit. God is the One who gives wisdom and enlightens our hearts to understand the gospel. Without the Lord empowering us and guiding us, our Bible study would be futile. Prayer, then, is not a formality to brush off or an unnecessary step to skip. Out of all of the tools and strategies we will learn together in this study, prayer is the most practical and effective thing we can do in our pursuit of rightly understanding, interpreting, and applying God's Word. We come to the only One who can illuminate our hearts and our minds to the truth of His Word and ask Him to do it, knowing that He will be faithful to answer those prayers (James 1:5, Matthew 7:7).

How can we pray as we approach God's Word? We can use the words of the Psalmist in Psalm 119:18, asking God to "Open my eyes so that I may contemplate wondrous things from your instruction." We can ask Him to help us understand the words we read, to show us Himself in the pages of Scripture, and to change us through it. We can ask Him to convict us through the Scriptures of the sin in our own hearts and empower us to turn and walk in the obedience to which He has called us therein. We can adore Him for who we have seen Him to be through the revelation of His Word, and we can thank Him for His faithfulness displayed in the pages of the Bible. We can confess our sins of which we have been convicted and ask Him for forgiveness. We can pray for the church to live as God's Word calls it to live. We can pray for our friends and neighbors to be changed by the gospel. We pray before we read Scripture, we pray while we are reading it, and we pray in response to it.

Use the space below to write a prayer asking for the Lord's help as you embark on this journey of studying God's Word.

“
Our God did not
leave us alone
in our sin
without hope.

Reading:
Romans 3:23,
Romans 6:23,
2 Corinthians 5:21

What is the Gospel?

As we begin to study the Bible, it is helpful for us to think through a very brief overview of the gospel message so that we are able to identify it throughout the story of Scripture. The message of the gospel in Scripture begins in Genesis as we are introduced to the all-powerful God of creation in chapter one. By chapter three, we witness the fall of humanity through Adam and Eve in the garden of Eden. Just three chapters into the grand narrative, and man has already descended into depravity. They doubted the Creator and sought to hide their sin. But in God's great mercy, He immediately provided a glimpse of what was to come. God gave a promise that there would come a day when the seed of the woman would rise up and crush the head of the serpent. The fall hurled the human race into sin, a reality from which no person is immune. Romans 3:23 emphasizes that we have all sinned, and Romans 6:23 makes it clear that the penalty for that sin is death.

Our God did not leave us alone in our sin without hope. That first veiled promise in Genesis 3 would point toward the coming of Jesus, the promised Messiah who would crush the head of that serpent and destroy the power of sin and death at the cross. Jesus entered the world as a humble Jewish baby born into the line of David. He lived the sinless life that we could not live, and He died the death that we deserved on the cross. He became sin for us so that we could be declared righteous before God (2 Corinthians 5:21). Through the death and resurrection of Jesus, we find life.

The gift of salvation is not something we can earn or achieve. There are no good works we can accomplish and no amount of religion that will save us. Salvation is received by grace through faith in the finished work of Jesus. He has paid the price that we never could on our own. In His overwhelming grace He

has pursued the hearts of His people. In His mercy He has not given us what we deserved. He simply asks us to accept the grace that He has given.

As believers, we now live in the hope that we have found in the gospel. We rest in His finished work of redemption and look forward to the return of Christ, the restoration of all that has been tainted by sin, and the joy of dwelling in the presence of our God forever.

Scripture to Reference

—

GENESIS 3

The fall of man takes place in the garden of Eden.

ROMANS 3:23

All have sinned.

ROMANS 6:23

The penalty for sin is death.

2 CORINTHIANS 5:21

Christ became sin for us so that we could be declared righteous before God.

Has there ever been a time that you have accepted God's gift of salvation? Describe it below.

How do you think an understanding of the message of the gospel helps us to understand the story of the Bible?

How should we live in response to the gospel and the gift of grace that we have been given?

Identifying the Gospel in Scripture

—

All of Scripture points to the gospel because all of Scripture points to Christ. If we do not read God's Word with the gospel in mind, we ignore the overarching purposes of God as recorded in His Word, and we run the risk of an interpretation that is moralistic or legalistic. As you read a passage of Scripture for how it reflects the gospel, consider how Old Testament passages anticipate the gospel and how New Testament passages reflect on the gospel. Consider ways that God's Word points to our need for the gospel, as well as the fruit of the gospel in the life of a believer and the future hope that the gospel guarantees.

WORKSHEET GUIDANCE:

- Underline or highlight in orange every reference to the sin nature and the consequences of sin.
- Underline or highlight in blue every reference to Jesus (Jesus, Christ, etc.).
- Underline or highlight in yellow every time the text shows what God does in the work of salvation.
- Underline or highlight in green how the gospel changes who we are and how we live.

Ephesians 2:1-10

1And you were dead in your trespasses and sins 2in which you previously walked
according to the ways of this world, according to the ruler of the power of the
air, the spirit now working in the disobedient. 3We too all previously lived among
them in our fleshly desires, carrying out the inclinations of our flesh and thoughts,
and we were by nature children under wrath as the others were also. 4But God,
who is rich in mercy, because of his great love that he had for us, 5made us alive
with Christ even though we were dead in trespasses. You are saved by grace! 6He
also raised us up with him and seated us with him in the heavens in Christ Jesus,
7so that in the coming ages he might display the immeasurable riches of his grace
through his kindness to us in Christ Jesus. 8For you are saved by grace through
faith, and this is not from yourselves; it is God's gift— 9not from works, so that
no one can boast. 10For we are his workmanship, created in Christ Jesus for good
works, which God prepared ahead of time for us to do.

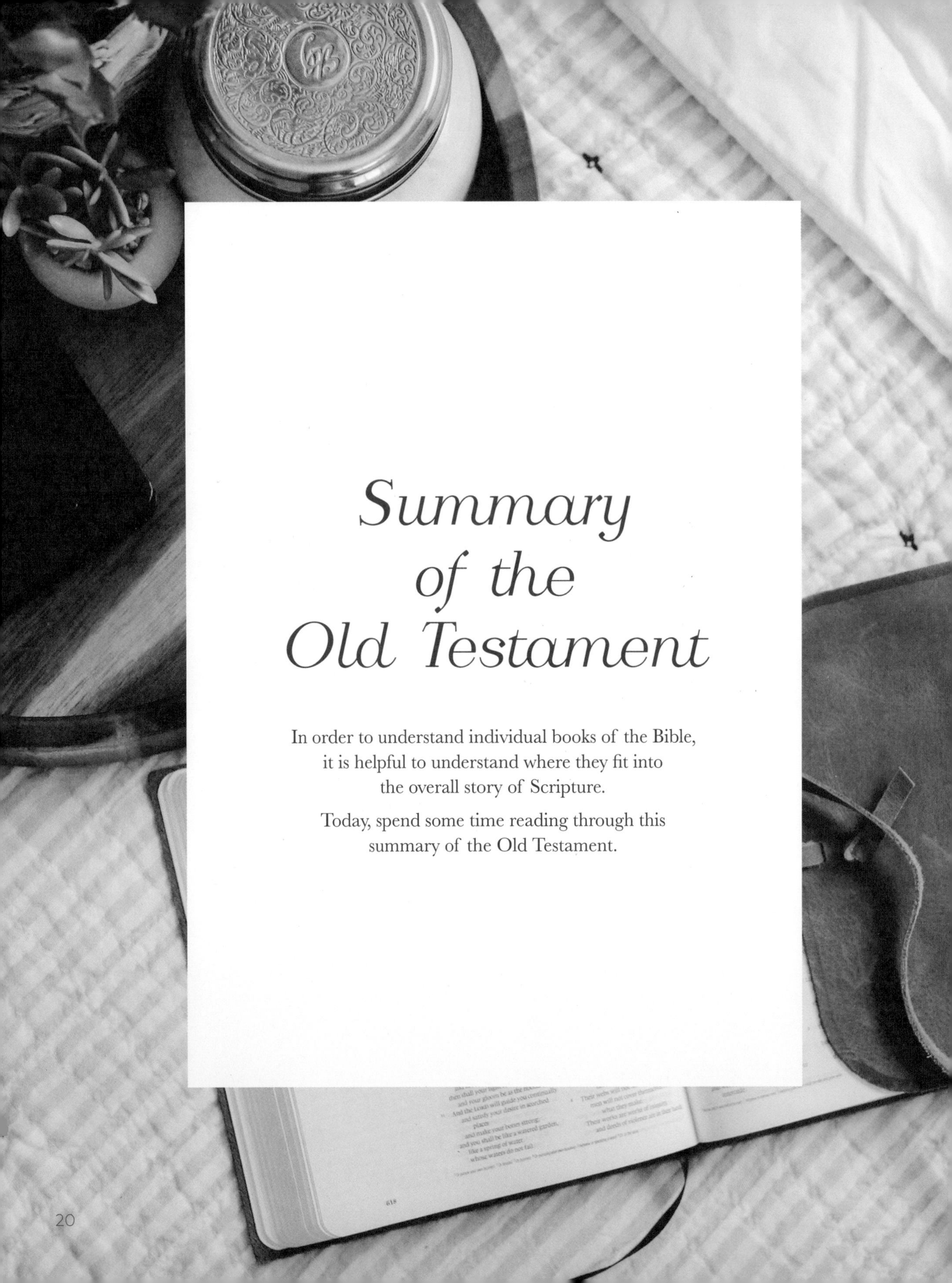

Summary of the Old Testament

In order to understand individual books of the Bible, it is helpful to understand where they fit into the overall story of Scripture.

Today, spend some time reading through this summary of the Old Testament.

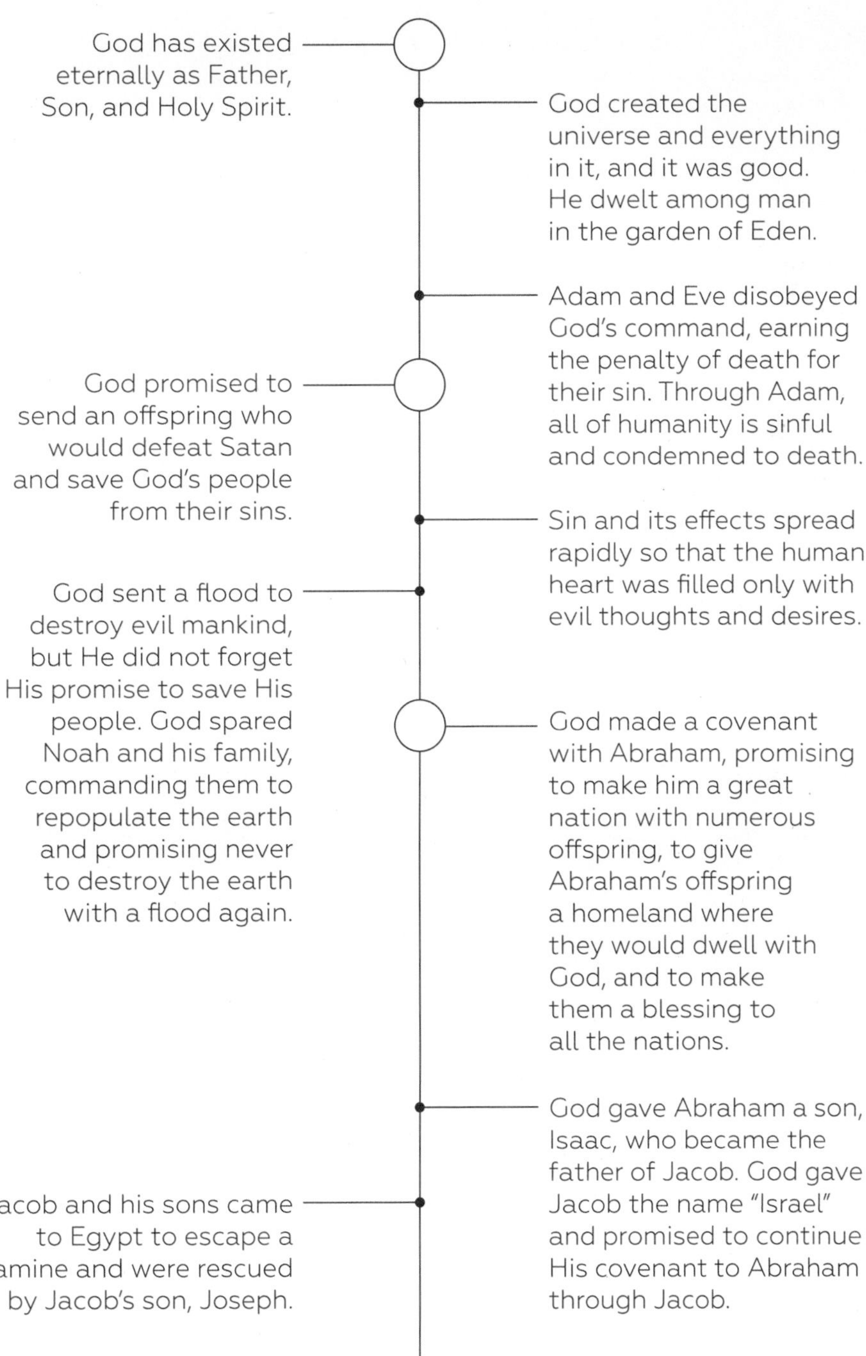
God has existed eternally as Father, Son, and Holy Spirit.
God created the universe and everything in it, and it was good. He dwelt among man in the garden of Eden.
Adam and Eve disobeyed God's command, earning the penalty of death for their sin. Through Adam, all of humanity is sinful and condemned to death.
God promised to send an offspring who would defeat Satan and save God's people from their sins.
Sin and its effects spread rapidly so that the human heart was filled only with evil thoughts and desires.
God sent a flood to destroy evil mankind, but He did not forget His promise to save His people. God spared Noah and his family, commanding them to repopulate the earth and promising never to destroy the earth with a flood again.
God made a covenant with Abraham, promising to make him a great nation with numerous offspring, to give Abraham's offspring a homeland where they would dwell with God, and to make them a blessing to all the nations.
God gave Abraham a son, Isaac, who became the father of Jacob. God gave Jacob the name "Israel" and promised to continue His covenant to Abraham through Jacob.
Jacob and his sons came to Egypt to escape a famine and were rescued by Jacob's son, Joseph.

The descendants of Jacob, known as the Israelites, multiplied to an enormous number in Egypt, a partial fulfillment of God's promise to give Abraham offspring more numerous than the stars.

A new Pharaoh of Egypt viewed the growing Israelite population as a threat, so he enslaved them and ordered that all baby boys born to Israelites were to be killed, but God spared a baby boy, Moses, whom He would raise up to deliver the Israelites from slavery.

God delivered the Israelites out of slavery in Egypt, instituting the Passover as a time to remember that God saved His people and to point forward to their redemption from sin.

God gave the Israelites the law, forming them into a nation, revealing how their lives should reflect His character as a blessing to the nations, and revealing their sin and their need for a savior.

The Israelites rebelled against God, but God remained faithful. He provided for and protected the Israelites, and after forty years, He brought them into the land of Canaan that He had promised to Abraham.

Israel continued to sin against God in the Promised Land, leading to cycles of Israel rebelling, God sending judgment to call them back to Himself, and then sending judges to deliver them when Israel repented.

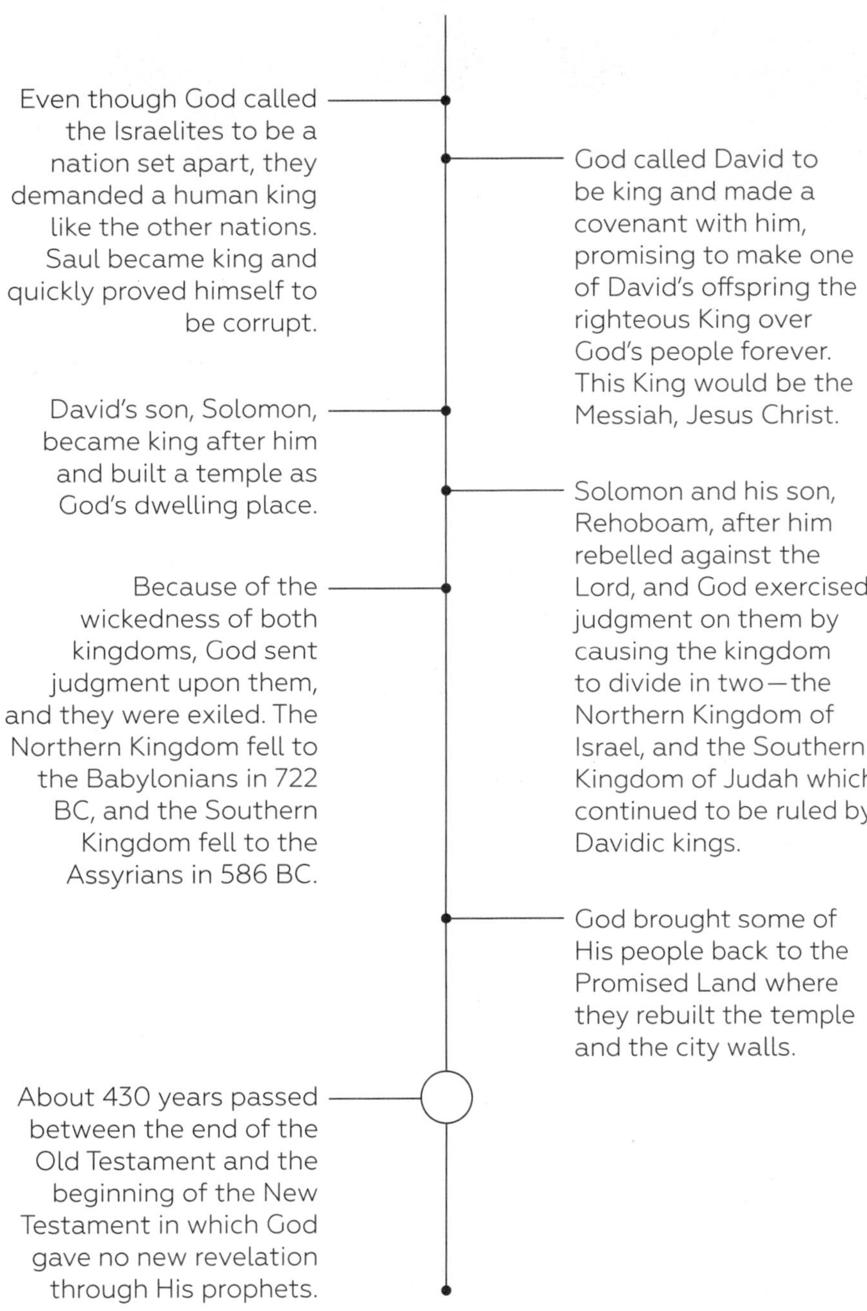

What part or parts of the Old Testament story are most familiar to you? Which parts are most unfamiliar? Go back, and re-read any portions of the summary that are less familiar.

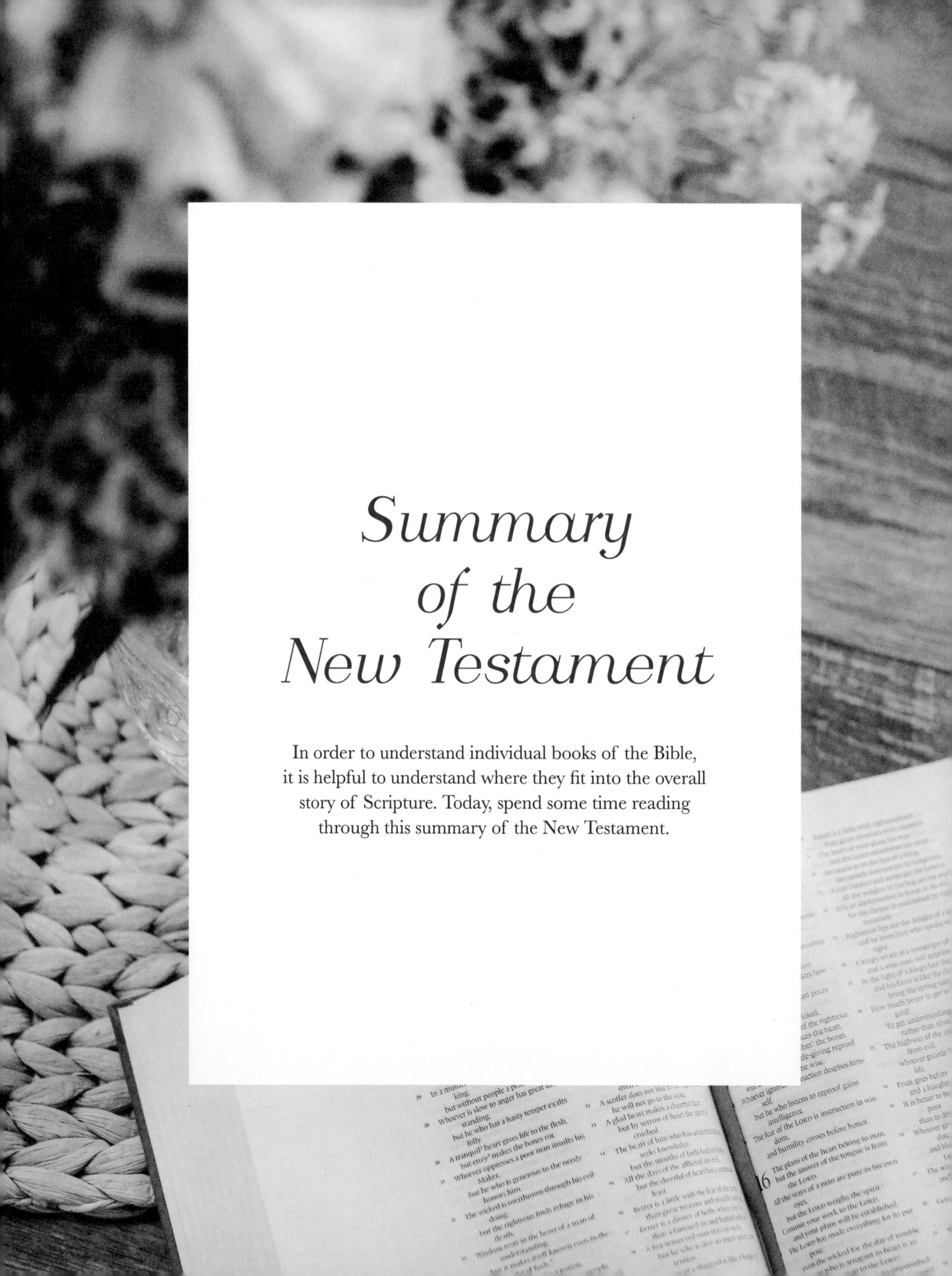

Summary of the New Testament

In order to understand individual books of the Bible, it is helpful to understand where they fit into the overall story of Scripture. Today, spend some time reading through this summary of the New Testament.

About 430 years after God last spoke through a prophet in the Old Testament, Jesus Christ, the promised Messiah and the son of God incarnate, was born in Bethlehem to the Virgin Mary.

John the Baptist began preparing the way for Jesus during his adult life by preaching a message of repentance in light of God's kingdom being at hand.

Jesus was baptized by John the Baptist around the age of thirty, at which point the Holy Spirit descended upon Him, and God the Father declared Him to be His beloved Son.

After His baptism, the Spirit led Jesus into the wilderness to be tempted by Satan for forty days. Jesus resisted temptation, proving Himself to be the true Son of God who succeeded in the face of temptation, whereas Israel failed to obey God in their forty years in the wilderness.

Jesus began His public ministry around the age of thirty, proclaiming the message of repentance and of the kingdom that has come near.

Jesus called His first disciples to leave their profession as fishermen and to follow Him.

Jesus' public ministry included teaching and performing miracles such as turning water into wine, healing diseases, casting out demons, and raising the dead, all of which point forward to the restoration He will bring at His second coming.

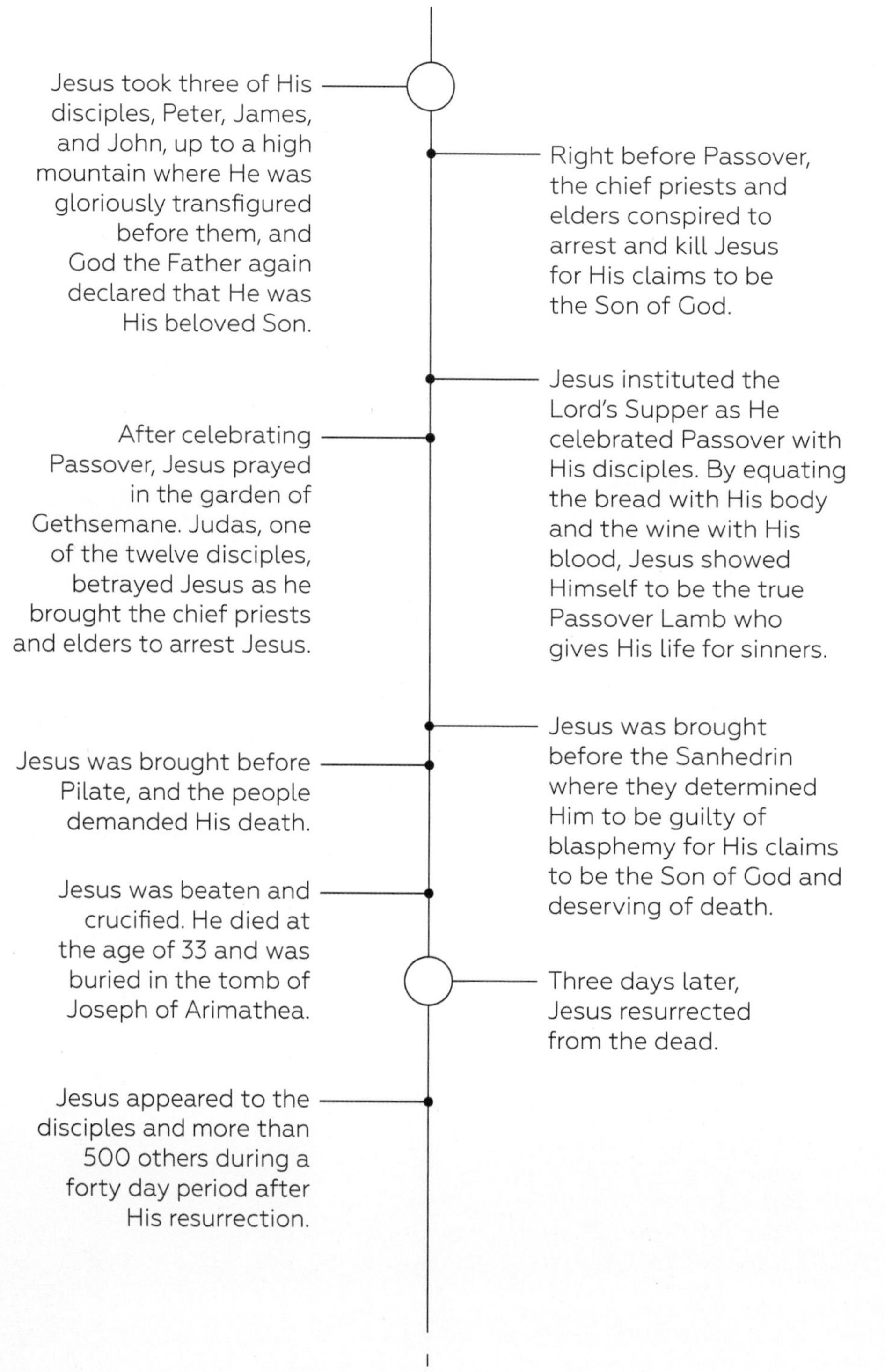

Jesus took three of His disciples, Peter, James, and John, up to a high mountain where He was gloriously transfigured before them, and God the Father again declared that He was His beloved Son.
Right before Passover, the chief priests and elders conspired to arrest and kill Jesus for His claims to be the Son of God.
Jesus instituted the Lord's Supper as He celebrated Passover with His disciples. By equating the bread with His body and the wine with His blood, Jesus showed Himself to be the true Passover Lamb who gives His life for sinners.
After celebrating Passover, Jesus prayed in the garden of Gethsemane. Judas, one of the twelve disciples, betrayed Jesus as he brought the chief priests and elders to arrest Jesus.
Jesus was brought before the Sanhedrin where they determined Him to be guilty of blasphemy for His claims to be the Son of God and deserving of death.
Jesus was brought before Pilate, and the people demanded His death.
Jesus was beaten and crucified. He died at the age of 33 and was buried in the tomb of Joseph of Arimathea.
Three days later, Jesus resurrected from the dead.
Jesus appeared to the disciples and more than 500 others during a forty day period after His resurrection.

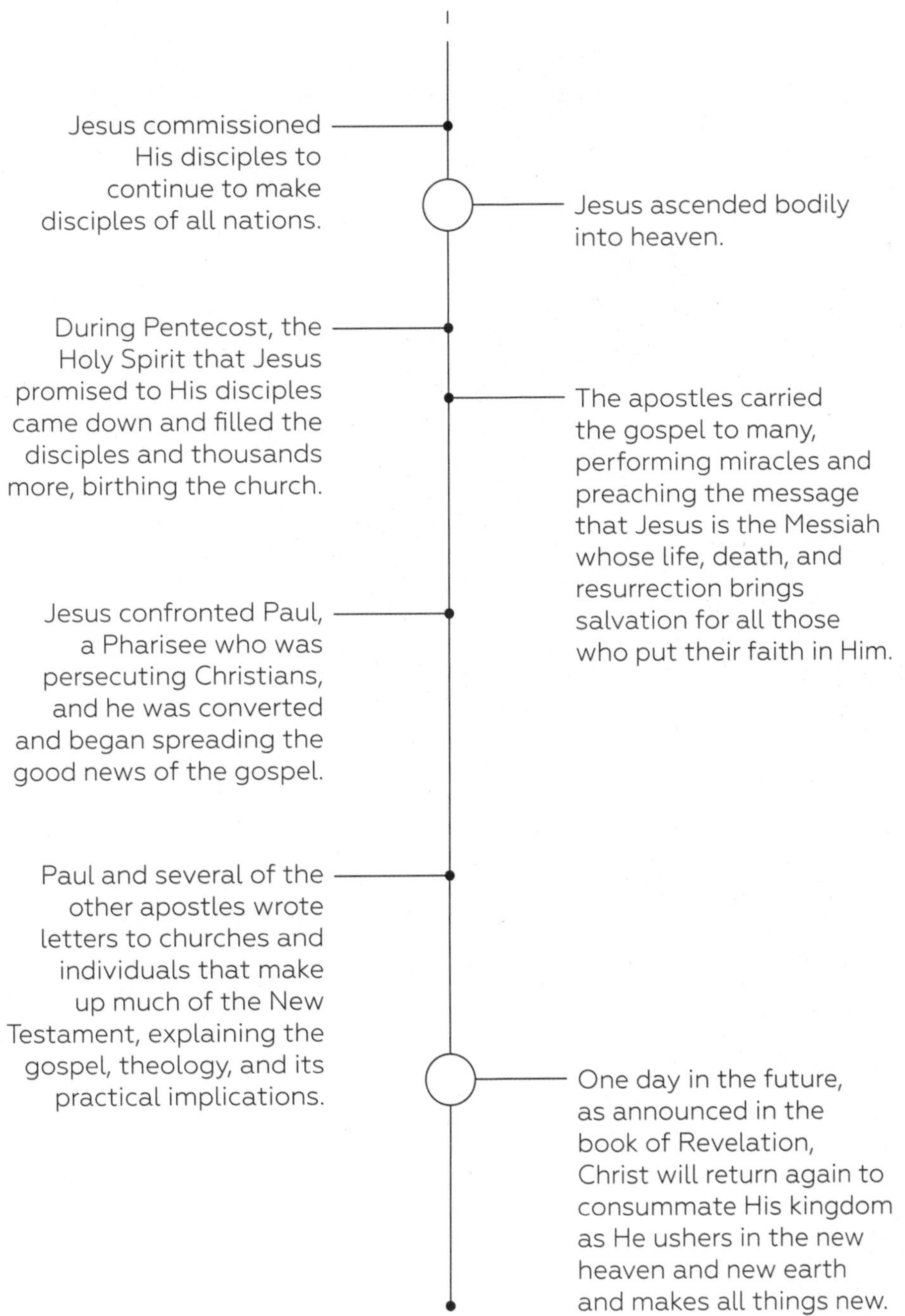

What part or parts of the New Testament story are most familiar to you? Which parts are most unfamiliar? Go back, and re-read any portions of the summary that are less familiar.

2 TIMOTHY 3:16-17

—

All Scripture is inspired by God and is profitable for teaching, for rebuking, for correcting, for training in righteousness, so that the man of God may be complete, equipped for every good work.

"
All of Scripture is about Jesus.

Reading:
Genesis 1–3,
2 Corinthians 5:8,
Revelation 21

The Metanarrative of Scripture

All of Scripture is about Jesus. All of the stories of Scripture point to the bigger story, the story of God's redemption. When we read the Bible, we should always seek to see how the text points to the promise of our Messiah and reflects our redemption in Christ. One simple way to identify that good news of the gospel in the Bible is by looking at the metanarrative of Scripture, which is the larger, overarching story of redemption that spans the entire Bible. The four categories that reflect different parts of the gospel story are creation, fall, redemption, and restoration.

CREATION

The first part of the story is creation. The book of Genesis reveals that everything originated from the only uncreated being, God Himself. He created the universe, and He called it good. He created man in His own image to be His ambassadors on earth. God dwelt among His people; He walked with them and communed with them. Not only did man not experience evil, he had no knowledge of it. No condemning shame. No whispers of anxiety. No fear of loss. All was well. His creative work continues as He sustains the universe and carries out every purpose of His will.

FALL

In Genesis 3, Adam and Eve disobeyed God, and sin entered the world. The consequences of sin are devastating and far reaching. Mankind, once pure and in the continual presence of the holy God, is now unclean and consumed by shame, and God sent them away from His presence. Sin always results in death, and it does not take long after the fall to see that the world is indeed dying. The effects of sin do not stop with Adam and Eve but are passed on to every generation. Within one generation, the sinful nature of man is put on horrific display as Cain murders his brother, Abel, out of jealousy. By Genesis 6, humanity has declined to the point that their wicked hearts are described as inclined only toward evil at all times. We don't have to look far to see the effects of sin in our world today. Whether it be poverty or natural disasters, disease or hatred, tragedy or shame, we cannot deny the devastation of the fall.

REDEMPTION

God does not leave us in our hopelessness. From the very beginning, God has been working to save His people. Jesus Christ accomplishes the work of redemption, saving us from our own sin, a task that we could never do on our own. Our promised Messiah, the One whom God promised from the very beginning, gave His own life to pay our penalty of death for our sins so that we might take on His righteousness and appear holy and blameless before the Almighty God. Even before Jesus took on human form, God's Word was pointing to Him. God uses flawed people throughout history to foreshadow and reflect the better Redeemer to come. The Old Testament points our hearts to the true Redeemer, Jesus Christ. Throughout our lives, the Holy Spirit applies the work of redemption as He sanctifies us, making us more and more holy and producing good fruit in our lives.

RESTORATION OR CONSUMMATION

God not only saves us from His wrath against sin, but He blesses us beyond anything we could ever think or imagine. Even after we have been justified by God's amazing grace, it is clear that we still live in a broken and fallen world. We still wrestle with the sinfulness of our hearts, and we are reminded every single day that things are not as they should be. Our God is a God who restores above and beyond what was lost, even though our own sin is the reason for the brokenness. God promises that Christ will return, and when He does, He will make all things new. Revelation 21 describes the restoration of Christ's kingdom in the new heaven and new earth, a place where sin and death and sadness are no more, and where God dwells with His people, a people glorified and made pure and holy by the blood of Christ.

All throughout the Bible, God's Word reveals glimmers of hope that remind us to set our hearts and our minds on the eternal promises of our gracious and merciful God. When we see the stories of the Bible in light of the bigger story, they take on new meaning and reveal to us more fully the beautiful character of our righteous God.

Write the metanarrative of Scripture in your own words.

How will understanding the metanarrative change the way you approach Scripture?

Understanding important background information enhances our studies.

Understanding Literary Genre & Type

The books of the Bible are pieces of literature, and just like with any literary work, it is important to understand the literary genre in order to correctly interpret the text. Genre refers to the category of literature into which a text falls. Genres vary in elements such as structure, tone, language, and content. The books of the Bible can be divided into six major categories: law, history, wisdom literature, prophecy, gospels, and epistles. Each of these genres falls into one of three larger types of literature: narrative, poetry, or discourse. While each book of the Bible generally falls into one of these categories, it is important to note that one book can contain multiple genres and types of literature. For example, the book of Jonah is considered a minor prophet, but it is written in the style of a historical narrative and has an entire chapter of poetry. The book of Luke falls under the category of Gospel, but the first chapter also contains a poetic song from Mary and prophecy from Zechariah, the father of John the Baptist. Even as we read, we must be aware of the stylistic elements of different genres so that we can properly interpret all of Scripture.

Knowing the genre of a book of the Bible before studying the text itself is vital to the way we understand, interpret, and apply a passage of Scripture. Some genres of biblical literature are wrought with figurative language, while others recount events as they occurred. Some parts of Scripture highlight promises, while others give general principles for living a godly life. Without an accurate understanding of how the biblical genres function, misinterpretation is highly likely, and although we may be tempted to jump into a book without any consideration for genre, understanding important background information enhances our studies.

Have you ever considered the role of genre when beginning to study a book of the Bible? Do you typically interpret Scripture with genre in mind, or do you tend to approach different books of the Bible in the same way?

How would knowing that one movie falls under the category of documentary while another is a fictional drama change your viewing experience? How would it impact the way you understand, interpret, and respond to them?

Just like movies and literary works, the books of the Bible cannot be properly understood apart from an understanding of their literary genre. How does this knowledge change the way you think about reading the Bible?

Genre in Scripture

OLD TESTAMENT

LAW

Genesis
Exodus
Leviticus
Numbers
Deuteronomy

HISTORY

Joshua
Judges
Ruth
1 Samuel
2 Samuel
1 Kings
2 Kings
1 Chronicles
2 Chronicles
Ezra
Nehemiah
Esther

WISDOM LITERATURE

Job
Psalm
Proverbs
Ecclesiastes
Song of Solomon

MAJOR PROPHETS

Isaiah
Jeremiah
Lamentations
Ezekiel
Daniel

MINOR PROPHETS

Hosea
Joel
Amos
Obadiah
Jonah
Micah
Nahum
Habakkuk
Zephaniah
Haggai
Zechariah
Malachi

INTERTESTAMENTAL PERIOD

NEW TESTAMENT

GOSPELS

Matthew
Mark
Luke
John

HISTORY

Acts

EPISTLES

Romans
1 Corinthians
2 Corinthians
Galatians
Ephesians
Philippians
Colossians
1 Thessalonians
2 Thessalonians
1 Timothy
2 Timothy
Titus
Philemon
Hebrews
James
1 Peter
2 Peter
1 John
2 John
3 John
Jude

PROPHECY

Revelation

Narrative: History, Law, & Gospels

—

A large portion of the Old Testament, as well as part of the five opening books of the New Testament, fall under the literary type of historical narrative. The books in this genre include the Old Testament books of the Law and of history, as well as the four Gospels and the historical book of Acts in the New Testament. Historical narrative recounts true, historical events in story form, typically in chronological order. When reading historical narrative, it is important to identify the plot line of the story itself while also considering how it falls into the bigger story of redemptive history as revealed in the metanarrative of Scripture.

While historical narrative recounts historical events, it will often omit details. Just like any storyteller, the biblical authors intentionally focus on specific elements of a historical event. It is important to understand that historical narratives will not include every word spoken or every action taken, and therefore we must not be quick to draw conclusions from what is not there, nor should we view omission as an error.

The first five books of the Bible are called the Pentateuch. While the Bible frequently refers to the first five books of the Bible as the Law, some books in the Pentateuch focus more on history, while others, such as the book of Leviticus and sections of Exodus and Deuteronomy, focus more specifically on the law code that God gave to the Israelites. These portions of Scripture are notorious for being difficult to read, but when we read them within the context of God's greater plan of redemption, we will see them in an entirely new light. God gave the law to Israel so that they could live as a people set apart to reflect God's character to the world. Time and time again, Israel failed to keep God's commandments, and so the Law not only serves to display God's holy character but also to reveal the sinfulness of humanity and our need for a savior, Jesus Christ. He came to perfectly fulfill the law where we could not, taking upon Himself our penalty for breaking it and giving us the reward of eternal life when we place our faith in Him. From the purity laws to the bloody descriptions of animal sacrifices, the Law points to Christ who is perfectly holy and who purifies us with His blood.

The four Gospels—Matthew, Mark, Luke, and John—are primarily historical narrative, but they also include sections of other types of literature, namely poetry and discourse, as well as sub-genres of literature, like parables. Parables are stories told to teach a moral lesson, and Jesus used parables to reveal things about Himself, His mission, and how His people should live in the world. Unlike historical narrative, parables are not intended to recount actual events but are typically fictional stories that poignantly illustrate an important point. Historical narratives sometimes communicate moral lessons, but we must exercise caution in looking to the characters in narratives as models to emulate. Just because an event or action is recorded in Scripture does not mean that God condones the behavior. The only sinless human in the Bible is Jesus Christ, and although other characters often display admirable traits, they also display sinful behavior, and we must not be too quick to blindly follow their examples. Sometimes a text will directly state whether someone's actions were honorable or sinful. Sometimes an author will use literary devices to highlight a character's sin or faith. Yet other times the text simply states events as they happened without any indication as to their morality.

The question we should ask as we approach historical narrative, and all of Scripture for that matter, is not, "How can I emulate these people?" but "What does this text reveal about God?" and "How should I live in response?"

Historical Narrative

WORKSHEET GUIDANCE:

This passage from the book of Genesis falls under the category of historical narrative. Read the passage below, and answer the following questions about its genre.

Genesis 11:1-9

1The whole earth had the same language and vocabulary. 2As people
migrated from the east, they found a valley in the land of Shinar and
settled there. 3They said to each other, “Come, let us make oven-fired
bricks.” (They used brick for stone and asphalt for mortar.) 4And they
said, “Come, let us build ourselves a city and a tower with its top in the
sky. Let us make a name for ourselves; otherwise, we will be scattered
throughout the earth.”
5Then the Lord came down to look over the city and the tower that the
humans were building. 6The Lord said, “If they have begun to do this
as one people all having the same language, then nothing they plan to
do will be impossible for them. 7Come, let’s go down there and confuse
their language so that they will not understand one another’s speech.”
8So from there the Lord scattered them throughout the earth, and they
stopped building the city. 9Therefore it is called Babylon, for there the
Lord confused the language of the whole earth, and from there the
Lord scattered them throughout the earth.

What are some elements of this passage that indicate that it is a historical narrative?

Make a list of all of the characters in the passage.

In your own words, summarize the plot of the narrative.

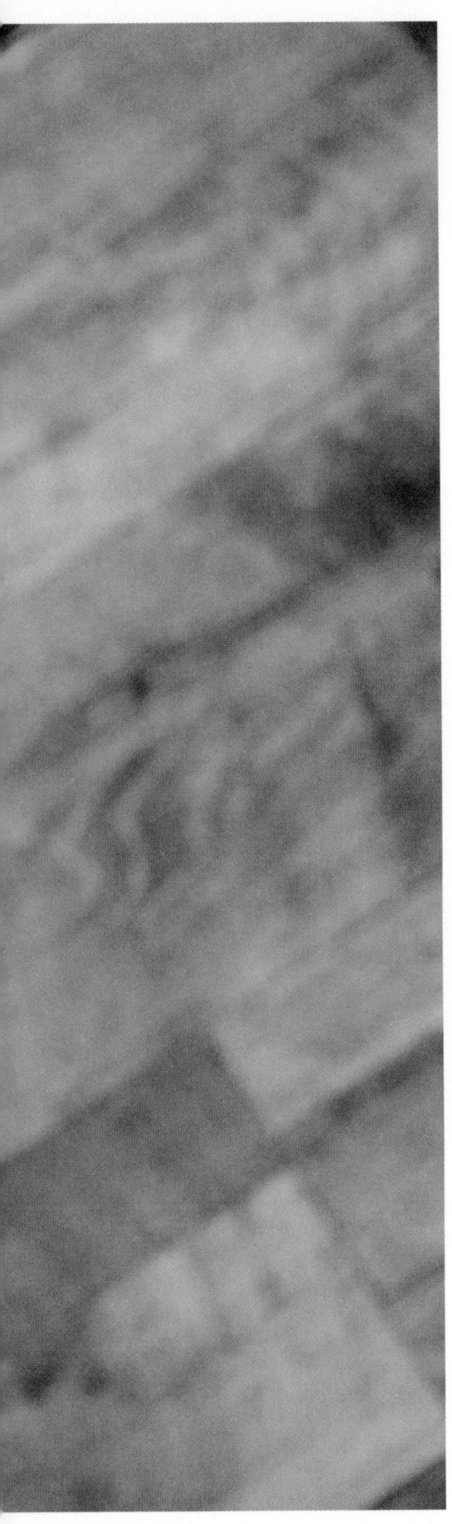

Poetry: Wisdom Literature

Much of Scripture is poetic. The books of poetry include Job, Psalms, Proverbs, Ecclesiastes, and Song of Solomon. These books also fall under the genre of wisdom literature because they give principles on how to live wisely in the world. Poetry uses figurative language to communicate complex emotions and ideas in a way that prose cannot. Unlike narrative, poetry is not intended to be taken literally but should be interpreted with a mind for the figurative language that expresses truths that the author wishes to communicate more abstractly.

When reading wisdom literature, it is also important to recognize the distinction between promises and principles. While much of Scripture contains absolute promises, much of the wisdom literature, such as the book of Proverbs, contains principles for godly living and the results they often produce, but they are not meant to be interpreted as promises that will always come true. For example, the well-known Proverbs 22:6 (ESV) that says, "Train up a child in the way he should go; even when he is old he will not depart from it," is not a promise that godly parenting will always lead to children who know and love the Lord, but it expresses a pattern that often, though not always, occurs in Christian households.

Poetry uses figurative language to communicate complex emotions and ideas in a way that prose cannot.

Figurative Language

Metaphor

Describing an object in a way that is not literally true in order to make a comparison

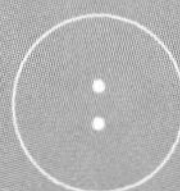

Simile

A comparison between two things using the word "like" or "as"

Hyperbole

Exaggeration for the sake of emphasis

Irony

When the opposite of what the reader expects to happen is what occurs

Imagery

The use of figurative or descriptive language that appeals to the senses

Personification

Giving a non-human thing human characteristics

Metonymy

Referring to something by using the name of something else to which it is related (ex: saying "the crown" to refer to a king or queen)

WORKSHEET GUIDANCE:

Read Psalm 42 below. Highlight or mark and label every instance of figurative language that you observe before answering the questions that follow.

1 As a deer longs for flowing streams, so I long
for you, God.
2 I thirst for God, the living God. When can
I come and appear before God?
3 My tears have been my food day and night,
while all day long people say to me, "Where
is your God?"
4 I remember this as I pour out my heart:
how I walked with many, leading the festive
procession to the house of God, with joyful
and thankful shouts.
5 Why, my soul, are you so dejected? Why are
you in such turmoil? Put your hope in God, for
I will still praise him, my Savior and my God.
6 I am deeply depressed; therefore I remember
you from the land of Jordan and the peaks of
Hermon, from Mount Mizar.
7 Deep calls to deep in the roar of your water-
falls; all your breakers and your billows have
swept over me.
8 The Lord will send his faithful love by day; his
song will be with me in the night—a prayer to
the God of my life.
9 I will say to God, my rock, "Why have you
forgotten me? Why must I go about in sorrow
because of the enemy's oppression?"
10 My adversaries taunt me, as if crushing
my bones, while all day long they say to me,
"Where is your God?"
11 Why, my soul, are you so dejected? Why are
you in such turmoil? Put your hope in God, for
I will still praise him, my Savior and my God.

How does the simile in verse one impact your understanding of the psalmist's emotional state?

What does the imagery in verse seven communicate about the psalmist?

What does the metaphor in verse nine reveal about God's character?

Psalm 34:13
AND RECITE
Psalm 34

Prophecy

The Old Testament major and minor prophets, as well as the book of Revelation, all fall under the category of prophetic literature. Each of these books was written by a prophet. A biblical prophet is someone who receives the Word of God directly and acts as His representative to speak His words to His people.

The Old Testament prophets primarily proclaim God's words to the Israelites both before and after the exile. When God brought His people out of slavery in Egypt, He made a covenant with them in the wilderness. God gave them His law, and they were to be His representatives to the world around them as they obeyed His commandments, but God's people and the kings who led them turned from Him and disobeyed His laws. God's Word in the Old Testament prophets includes accusations against the people for the sins they have committed against God, as well as calls for them to repent from their sin and return to the Lord and His commands. It includes God's impending judgment for their sin, as well as the promise of His mercy and forgiveness if they repent. The prophets are also filled with promises of a renewed creation under the rule of a Messianic King, who is Jesus Christ.

The New Testament prophetic book, the book of Revelation, is the account of a vision that God revealed to John through His angel while John was on the island of Patmos. This vision speaks about the end times and the future, second coming of Jesus Christ when He will usher in the new heaven and the new earth.

One very important element of prophetic literature is its use of imagery. Prophetic books paint vivid word pictures in order to communicate truths about God, humanity, and redemption. It is important to remember that imagery is a type of figurative language, and the descriptions in the prophetic books should not always be taken literally. For example, Isaiah 55:12 points forward to the second coming of Christ, and it speaks of the trees clapping their hands as the people of God are led into the new creation. This statement is not meant to indicate that the trees will literally sprout hands and become animated, but the language paints a figurative picture of the glorious day when the curse will be lifted from creation, and mourning will be turned to rejoicing. Most of the Old Testament prophets are written in poetry, and the same guidelines for interpreting figurative language in the wisdom literature can be applied to prophets. Even though the book of Revelation is largely prose, there are portions of poetry, and vivid, symbolic imagery throughout.

WORKBOOK PAGE

The book of Hosea was written to Ephraim, which is the Northern Kingdom of Israel, just before its exile in which God's judgment came upon them for their idolatry and disobedience to the covenant, which is the Law. In this minor prophet, God warns of the coming judgment, calls Israel to repentance, and points to a time after the exile when He will show them mercy once again and gather His people to Himself.

WORKSHEET GUIDANCE:

Read and annotate the passage on the next page from Hosea 11 using the prompts below before answering the questions that follow:

— Imagery: Underline any instances of imagery.

- Highlight or mark accusations that God brings against His people in orange.
- Highlight or mark God's judgment against sin in yellow.
- Highlight or mark repentance or returning to the Lord in green.
- Highlight or mark God's mercy, redemption, and restoration in blue.

Hosea 11:1-11

1 When Israel was a child, I loved him, and
out of Egypt I called my son.

2 Israel called to the Egyptians even as Israel
was leaving them. They kept sacrificing to the
Baals and burning offerings to idols.

3 It was I who taught Ephraim to walk,
taking them by the hand, but they never
knew that I healed them.

4 I led them with human cords, with ropes
of love. To them I was like one who eases
the yoke from their jaws; I bent down to give
them food.

5 Israel will not return to the land of Egypt
and Assyria will be his king, because they
refused to repent.

6 A sword will whirl through his cities;
it will destroy and devour the bars of his
gates, because of their schemes.

7 My people are bent on turning from me.
Though they call to him on high, he will
not exalt them at all.

8 How can I give you up, Ephraim?
How can I surrender you, Israel? How can I
make you like Admah? How can I treat you
like Zeboiim? I have had a change of heart;
my compassion is stirred!

9 I will not vent the full fury of my anger; I will
not turn back to destroy Ephraim. For I am
God and not man, the Holy One among you;
I will not come in rage.

10 They will follow the Lord; he will roar like
a lion. When he roars, his children will come
trembling from the west.

11 They will be roused like birds from Egypt
and like doves from the land of Assyria.
Then I will settle them in their homes.
This is the Lord's declaration.

How does the imagery of a child learning to walk in verse three fully communicate God's love for Israel?

What sin does God accuse Israel of committing?

What are the results of God's compassion in this passage?

"
It is incredibly valuable to read the letter as a whole, from start to finish.

Discourse: Epistles

Discourse is a type of literature that is meant to be read or spoken aloud in order to provide instruction. Sections of the Bible that are written in this literary type include the sermons of Jesus in the Gospels, the speeches of Peter and Paul in the book of Acts, and most of the Epistles. Out of the 27 books of the New Testament, 22 of them fall under the genre of epistle. An epistle is a letter written by an apostle of Jesus Christ or a close associate of an apostle. These letters are written to local churches or individuals in the early church, and they typically focus on presenting the message of the gospel and communicating how believers should practically apply it in their own lives. The content of the letters depends largely on the experiences of the individuals or churches to which they are written. Some letters offer encouragement in the midst of persecution, while others confront sin issues in a church that need to be addressed. Regardless of the specific focus, each of the Epistles gives the believer valuable principles for living the Christian life in light of the life, death, resurrection, and future return of Jesus Christ.

Like most letters, the structure of epistles includes an introduction, body, and conclusion. The intro typically begins with an opening greeting, which introduces the author, identifies the recipients, and includes some form of salutation. The standard letter form includes a prayer or expression of thanksgiving in the introduction. Next, the bulk of the letter is contained in the letter's body, which often includes a presentation of the gospel, followed by practical application specific to the audience's particular context. Finally, epistles end with a conclusion, which may include greetings to specific individuals or groups of people, final exhortations, and doxology, which is a prayer of worship, or a benediction, which is a blessing of peace.

Epistles, like other letters, are intended to be read as a whole. Even though we will likely study a smaller portion of a letter in depth before continuing on to the next section, it is incredibly valuable to read the letter as a whole, from start to finish, at least once in order to understand the overall flow of the epistle's content. If we will take the time to read the letter in its entirety, we can more clearly understand the content of individual passages as we consider them in light of the whole.

Structure of an Epistle

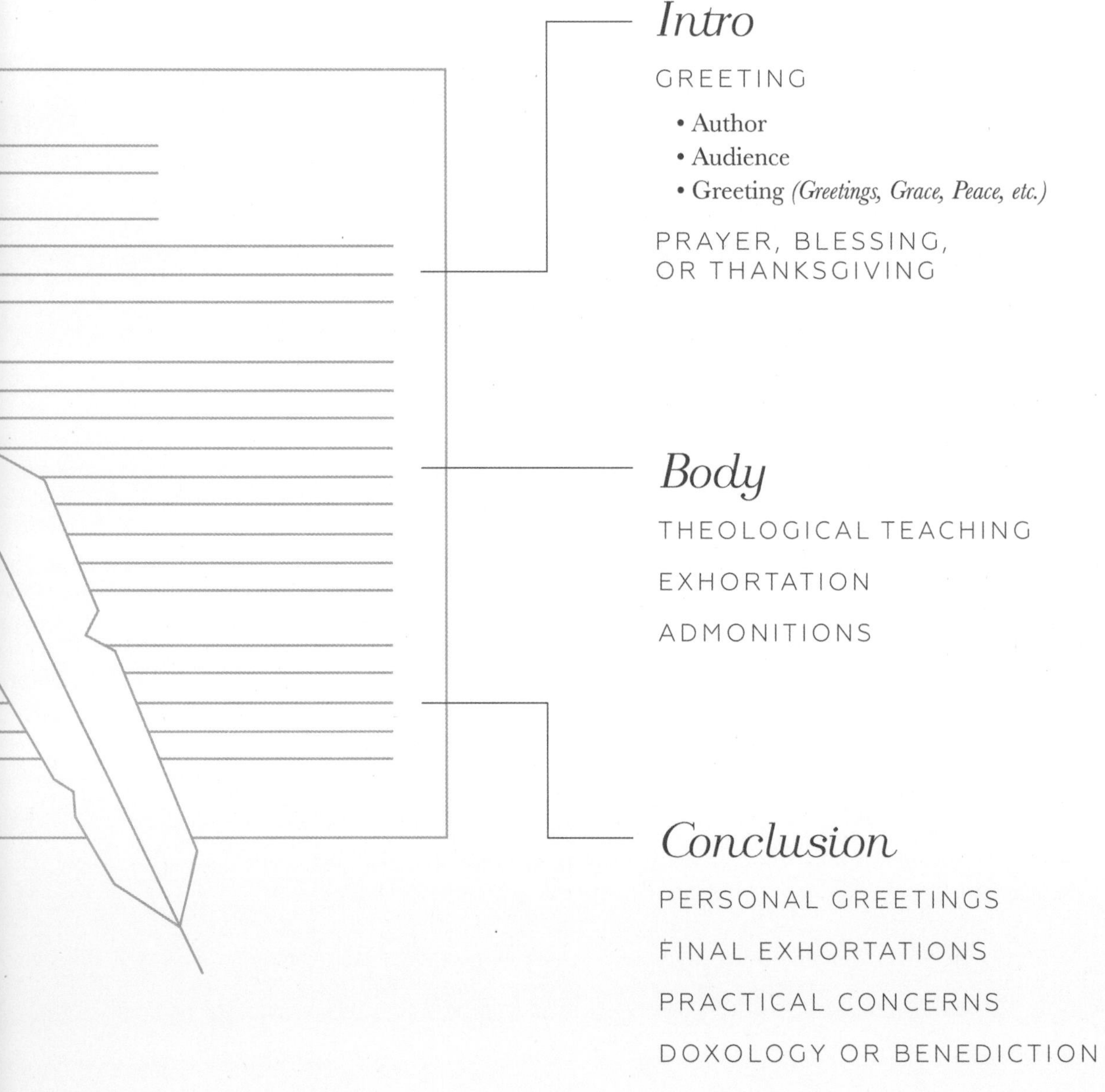

Epistles

WORKSHEET GUIDANCE:

In the introduction to the book of Philippians below, mark and label the different elements of epistolary structure that are present.

Philippians 1:1-11

1 Paul and Timothy, servants of Christ Jesus:

To all the saints in Christ Jesus who are in Philippi, including the overseers and deacons.

2 Grace to you and peace from God our Father and the Lord Jesus Christ.

3 I give thanks to my God for every remembrance of you, 4 always praying with joy for all of you
in my every prayer, 5 because of your partnership in the gospel from the first day until now. 6 I am
sure of this, that he who started a good work in you will carry it on to completion until the day of
Christ Jesus. 7 Indeed, it is right for me to think this way about all of you, because I have you in
my heart, and you are all partners with me in grace, both in my imprisonment and in the defense
and confirmation of the gospel. 8 For God is my witness, how deeply I miss all of you with the
affection of Christ Jesus. 9 And I pray this: that your love will keep on growing in knowledge and
every kind of discernment, 10 so that you may approve the things that are superior and may be
pure and blameless in the day of Christ, 11 filled with the fruit of righteousness that comes through
Jesus Christ to the glory and praise of God.

WORKSHEET GUIDANCE:

In this section from the body of Philippians, mark and label the different elements of epistolary structure that are present.

Philippians 2:1-11

1 If, then, there is any encouragement in Christ, if any consolation of love, if any fellowship with
the Spirit, if any affection and mercy, 2 make my joy complete by thinking the same way, having the
same love, united in spirit, intent on one purpose. 3 Do nothing out of selfish ambition or conceit,
but in humility consider others as more important than yourselves. 4 Everyone should look not to
his own interests, but rather to the interests of others.

5 Adopt the same attitude as that of Christ Jesus,
6 who, existing in the form of God, did not
consider equality with God as something to
be exploited.

7 Instead he emptied himself by assuming the
form of a servant, taking on the likeness of humanity. And when he had come as a man,
8 he humbled himself by becoming obedient to
the point of death—even to death on a cross.

9 For this reason God highly exalted him and
gave him the name that is above every name,
10 so that at the name of Jesus every knee will
bow—in heaven and on earth and under the
earth—

11 and every tongue will confess that Jesus
Christ is Lord, to the glory of God the Father.

WORKSHEET GUIDANCE:

In this section from the conclusion of Philippians, mark and label the different elements of epistolary structure that are present.

Philippians 4:21-23

21 Greet every saint in Christ Jesus. The brothers who are with me send you greetings.

22 All the saints send you greetings, especially those who belong to Caesar's household.

23 The grace of the Lord Jesus Christ be with your spirit.

Scripture Memory

2 CORINTHIANS 1:20

—

For every one of God's promises is "Yes" in him. Therefore, through him we also say "Amen" to the glory of God.

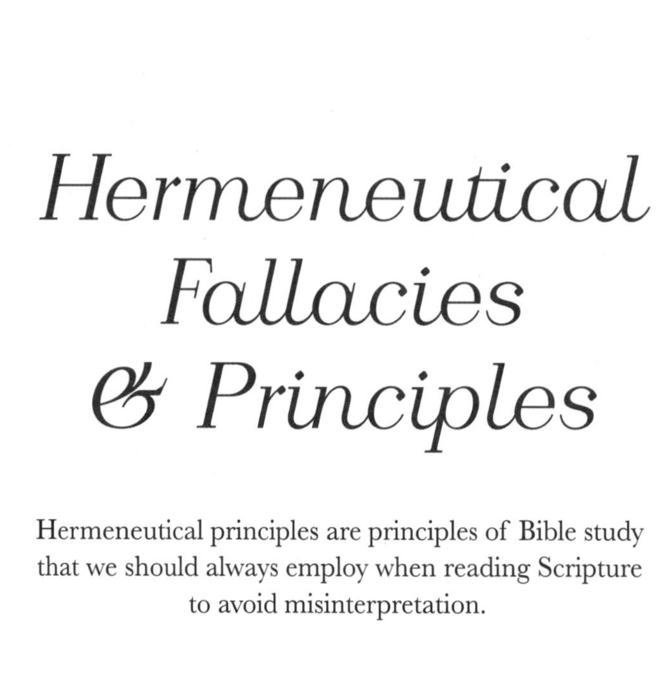

Hermeneutical Fallacies & Principles

Hermeneutical principles are principles of Bible study that we should always employ when reading Scripture to avoid misinterpretation.

— HERMENEUTICAL —

FALLACY	PRINCIPLE
Reading out of context	Always consider the historical, literary, and biblical context.
Adding to or taking away from God's Word	Seek to understand Scripture as it is written without any personal biases.
Eisegesis: Reading a meaning into the text	Exegesis: Draw out the intended meaning of the text.
Interpreting Scripture through the lens of our own cultural experience	Interpret Scripture through the lens of the cultural context of the original audience.
Forming a doctrine from a single verse	Allow Scripture to interpret Scripture.
Allegorizing a passage that is not meant to be allegorized	Remember that more often than not, the obvious interpretation is the correct interpretation.
Asking, "What does the text mean to me?"	Ask, "what did the text mean to the original audience?" before attempting to apply it to yourself.

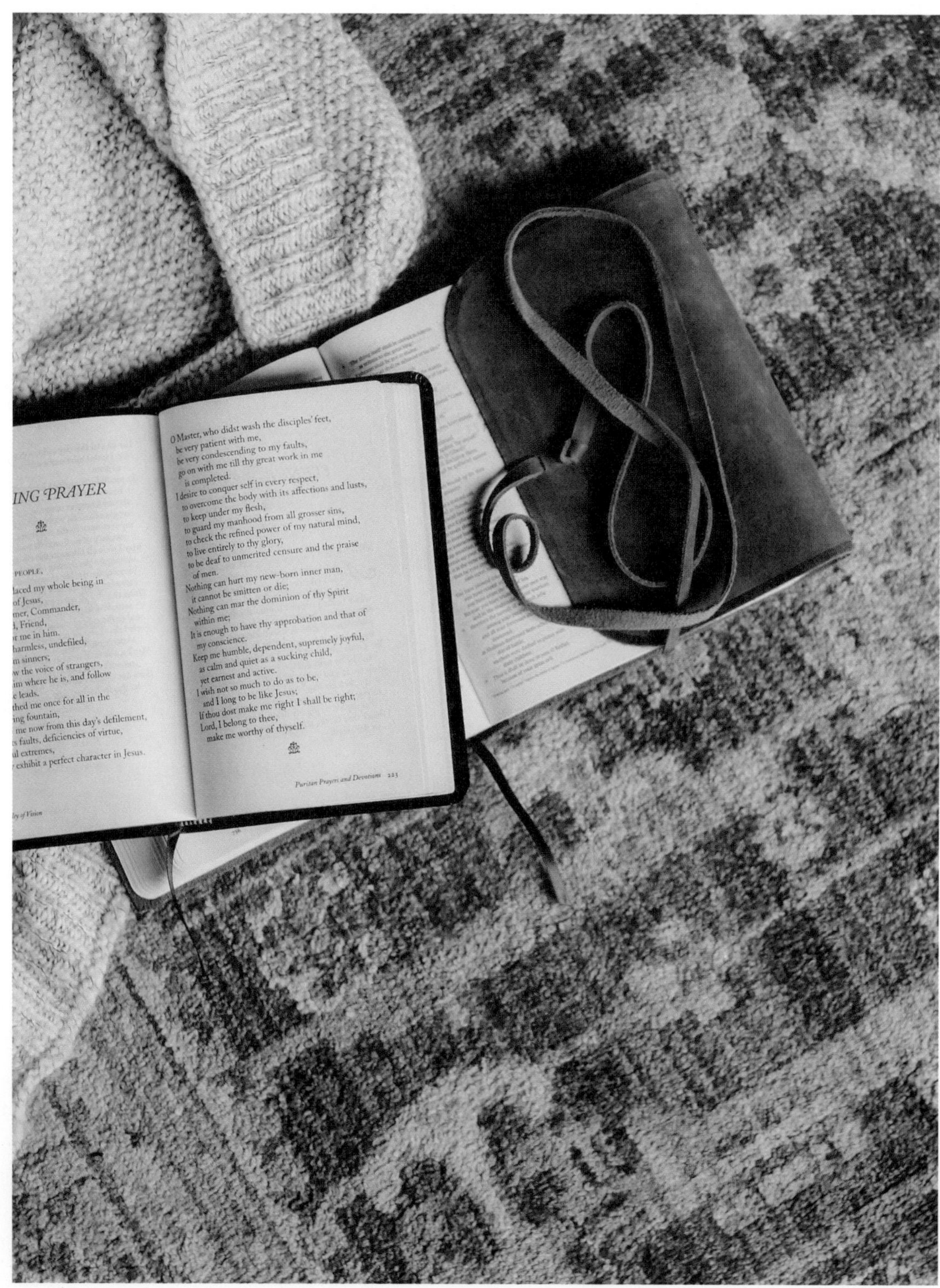

O Master, who didst wash the disciples' feet,
be very patient with me,
be very condescending to my faults,
go on with me till thy great work in me
is completed.
I desire to conquer self in every respect,
to overcome the body with its affections and lusts,
to keep under my flesh,
to guard my manhood from all grosser sins,
to check the refined power of my natural mind,
to live entirely to thy glory,
to be deaf to unmerited censure and the praise
of men.
Nothing can hurt my new-born inner man,
it cannot be smitten or die;
Nothing can mar the dominion of thy Spirit
within me;
It is enough to have thy approbation and that of
my conscience.
Keep me humble, dependent, supremely joyful,
as calm and quiet as a sucking child,
yet earnest and active.
I wish not so much to do as to be,
and I long to be like Jesus;
If thou dost make me right I shall be right;
Lord, I belong to thee,
make me worthy of thyself.
Puritan Prayers and Devotions 223

Introduction to the Inductive Method

We must not ask, "What does this passage mean to me?" until we first understand, "What did this passage mean to its original audience?"

The Inductive Method of Bible study provides tools needed to search for the intended meaning of the text by understanding it in its appropriate context. We must not ask, "What does this passage mean to me?" until we first understand, "What did this passage mean to its original audience?" When we see the intended meaning of a passage, we learn universal truths about who God is—truth that holds true throughout all time, all cultures, all circumstances, and for all people. It is then, when we see God for who He is, that the truth in the Bible changes how we live.

The inductive method has three main stages: comprehension, interpretation, and application. However, before we jump into the steps of this method, it is helpful to orient ourselves to the setting of the specific book of the Bible. Before studying any book of the Bible, it is worthwhile to gather background information in order to understand the historical context in which the book was written. Some information can be found in the text itself, while other information will require the use of commentaries or other resources. One good place to find this information is in the introduction to each book of the Bible in the ESV Study Bible. In your reading, try to answer the following five archaeological questions:

1. *Who wrote the book?* Knowing the author of a book of the Bible helps us to understand the vantage point from which the book was written and can shed light on topics that the author discusses or arguments that he makes. As you research the author of the book, look for information such as the author's occupation, family background, and personal history.

2. *Who was the audience?* A good communicator tailors his writing to his audience, so it is important to understand the author's intended audience. Consider things like the audience's past and present circumstances and religious backgrounds. As you learn about the original readers of the book you are studying, try to put yourselves in their shoes and read the book from their vantage point, remembering that the text cannot mean anything now that it could not have meant to its original audience.
3. *When was it written?* The time period in which a book of the Bible was written has a huge impact on the content of the book and on how the reader should interpret it. Oftentimes something that is extremely puzzling or confusing finds a clear explanation in the cultural practices of the day. Ask yourself what historical or cultural circumstances give light to the meaning of the book and where the events of the book fall in redemptive history.
4. *What was the purpose of the book?* Every author has a purpose for their writing, and the biblical authors are no exception. Knowing the purpose of a book provides a framework for understanding the book's meaning. Books may be written, for example, to give a historical account of God's work of redemption in history, to encourage or exhort a church, or to call God's people to repentance.
5. *What is the genre of the book?* Just like any piece of literature, the books of the Bible fall into specific genres. The genre of a book determines the style in which the author will write, what information he includes or omits, and whether he will write using literal or figurative language. If we do not understand the elements of the genre of a book we are reading, we will be very likely to misinterpret what God is communicating through the author. As you research the genre of a book, try to identify the genre and what elements of that genre are important to know in order to understand the book.

You may feel eager to jump right into the text, and perhaps these steps seem unnecessary and time consuming, but the time you spend working to gain a deeper understanding of God's Word is never wasted. The hard work of studying the Bible reaps benefits of eternal value as you behold God for who He is and so are sanctified and transformed into His image.

Understanding Historical Context

WORKSHEET GUIDANCE:

In order to practice the inductive method, we will be using the book of 1 Peter. Use a study Bible, the internet, or other resources to fill out the chart below with any helpful information about each of the five categories for 1 Peter. Consider the following questions when completing the chart:

1. Who wrote the book? What is important to know about the author?
2. Who was the audience? What were their circumstances? Their religious and cultural backgrounds?
3. When was it written? When is the book set? What historical or cultural circumstances are important to know in order to understand the book?
4. What was the purpose of the book?
5. What is the genre of the book? What are the elements of this genre that are important to know in order to understand the book?

AUTHOR	AUDIENCE	DATE	PURPOSE	GENRE

Observation & Comprehension

—

Once you have gained some understanding of the context of the book, you are ready to jump into the text. The first step of the inductive method is comprehension or observation. In the comprehension phase, you are asking the question, "What does the text say?" In this initial phase, your goal should not be to determine the meaning of the text or to determine how it applies to your own life but simply to understand the basic line of thought of the text by observing details in the writing.

One of the most helpful and most difficult parts of the comprehension phase is that it forces us to slow down. It can be easy to quickly read through a passage of Scripture, decide what it means, and apply it to our own lives, believing that we know what it says and what it means. However, when we take the time to carefully observe what is going on in the text, we see things we would not be likely to notice in an initial reading. Being good stewards of God's Word by carefully working through the text helps us to understand the Scripture more clearly and more fully know the God whom His Word reveals.

As you approach the comprehension phase, work through the following steps:

Read the text in its entirety from start to finish at least once.

The books of the Bible, with the exception, perhaps, of the Psalms and Proverbs, were intended to be read as a whole. If you were to pick up a book or a letter, choose a line in the middle, and try to find something meaningful for your life, it would likely not make much sense. You have to read what comes before and after in order to understand what that line really means. The same applies for the books of the Bible. Reading the text as a whole helps reveal the overarching flow of thought in the book, which in turn gives light to the meaning of individual passages and verses.

Read the text repetitively.

The Bible was written in times, cultures, and languages that are very different from our own, so you might not catch everything that the author is trying to communicate on the first read. Repetitive reading helps us pick up on the message of the text as we build upon our knowledge with each consecutive reading. Repetitive reading also helps us to hide God's Word in our hearts, a practice that transforms us to look more and more like Jesus. Listening to the text while you are getting ready in the morning, driving to work, or doing the dishes is a great way to read repetitively.

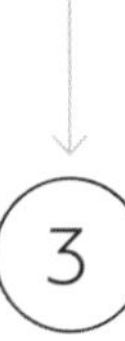

3

Read back through smaller portions of the text and mark it using a system that works for you.

Work through the book verse by verse, studying a chapter or a section of verses in depth before moving on to the next section. It is helpful to periodically read or listen through the entire book again in order to remind you of the context of your current set of verses. Bible marking pens and highlighters from The Daily Grace Co. are great tools for annotation. If you don't like to mark in your Bible, print out a copy of the text from a website like *www.biblegateway.com*. You can copy and paste it into a word processor and double space the text to give yourself plenty of room to annotate.

Mark the following elements in the text:

- Key or repeated words and ideas
- Key themes
- Transition words (Ex: therefore, but, because, if/then, likewise, etc...)
- Lists
- Comparisons & Contrasts
- Commands
- Unfamiliar words (Look these up in a dictionary.)
- Questions you have about the text (You will explore these questions in the interpretation phase.)

As you carefully read and annotate the passage, you should begin to understand what the author is communicating. As tempting as it may be, do not skip this step. The knowledge you gain from this step will ground and enhance your interpretation and application of the text.

How is the inductive method different from the way you have read the Bible in the past?

Are any parts of the inductive method confusing or intimidating to you?

How do you think the inductive method will be beneficial in your understanding of Scripture?

Understanding the Text as a Whole

WORKSHEET GUIDANCE:

Read the book of 1 Peter from start to finish at least once, and then make an outline of the letter in the space below. When creating your outline, consider elements like the letter's intro, body, and conclusion, but also consider more specific content within these larger sections. Your outline should give you an overview of the basic flow, argument, and content of the letter. If your Bible contains section headers, go to *www.biblegateway.com*, and use the settings button to remove headers.

How does the structure of the text impact your understanding of its message?

Read through 1 Peter again, and fill out the chart below as you read, noting key themes of the book, key verses, and any questions you have or things you find confusing.

After you have completed the chart, answer the questions that follow.

THEMES	KEY VERSES	QUESTIONS

What is the tone of the book of 1 Peter? How does the tone contribute to the overall purpose and argument of the book?

What is the big idea of the book of 1 Peter that runs from beginning to end? What is the main point that Peter is communicating?

Annotation

WORKSHEET GUIDANCE:

Read through the following passage from the book of 1 Peter, and then annotate it using the key below.

It may be most helpful to make one pass of the text for each individual element before moving on to the next.

- Highlight or underline key or repeated words in pink.
- Highlight or underline key themes in purple.
- Circle transition words.
- Write lists in the margins of the text.
- Highlight or underline comparisons & contrasts in blue.
- Highlight or underline commands in green.
- Write unfamiliar words and their definitions in the chart at the end of the text.
- Write questions about the passage in the chart at the end of the text.

1 Peter 2:1-12

[1]Therefore, rid yourselves of all malice, all
deceit, hypocrisy, envy, and all slander. [2]Like
newborn infants, desire the pure milk of the
word, so that by it you may grow up into your
salvation, [3]if you have tasted that the Lord is
good. [4]As you come to him, a living stone—
rejected by people but chosen and honored
by God— [5]you yourselves, as living stones,
a spiritual house, are being built to be a holy
priesthood to offer spiritual sacrifices accept-
able to God through Jesus Christ.

[6]For it stands in Scripture:

> See, I lay a stone in Zion,
> a chosen and honored cornerstone,
> and the one who believes in him
> will never be put to shame.

[7]So honor will come to you who believe; but
for the unbelieving,

> The stone that the builders
> rejected—
> this one has become the cornerstone,

[8]and

> A stone to stumble over,
> and a rock to trip over.

They stumble because they disobey the word;
they were destined for this.

[9]But you are a chosen race, a royal priesthood, a holy nation, a people for his possession, so that you may proclaim the praises of
the one who called you out of darkness into
his marvelous light. [10]Once you were not a
people, but now you are God's people; you
had not received mercy, but now you have
received mercy.

[11]Dear friends, I urge you as strangers and
exiles to abstain from sinful desires that wage
war against the soul. [12]Conduct yourselves
honorably among the Gentiles, so that when
they slander you as evildoers, they will observe
your good works and will glorify God on the
day he visits.

UNFAMILIAR WORDS	QUESTIONS ABOUT THE TEXT

What new things did you observe that you did not notice after an initial reading?

Were any of your questions from your initial readings of 1 Peter resolved after annotating the text? Did any new questions arise?

Literary Context

Some of our biggest interpretation errors occur because we read a verse out of context. Verses of the Bible are not meant to be read in isolation but as part of larger passages and books, with perhaps the exception of the Proverbs. Therefore, we should not attempt to interpret or apply a Bible verse without understanding it in its literary context. Literary context includes how a verse fits into the verses, chapter, and rest of the book surrounding it. We should always make sure we identify who is speaking and whom the speaker is addressing. It is also important to understand the point that the author is trying to make in the passage as a whole and how the individual verse fits into the larger argument. If the verse is a quotation from a character, we must consider whether or not the author condones the behavior of the character and if the verse is meant to tell us what to do or to simply tell us what happened.

Consider Philippians 4:13 printed below, and then answer the question that follows.

"I am able to do all things through him who strengthens me."

Based on reading this verse alone, what does its meaning appear to be?

Now read Philippians 4:10-14 to gain a picture of the literary context of Philippians 4:13, and then answer the questions below.

Who is speaking in Philippians 4:13?

To whom is the speaker addressing?

What is the speaker talking about in Philippians 4:10-14?

How is the point that the speaker makes in Philippians 4:13 related to the rest of the argument?

Based on the literary context, what is the meaning of Philippians 4:13? How does it differ from how you would have interpreted it if read in isolation?

Ask the question, "What would the text have meant to the original audience?"

Interpretation

After you answer the question, "What does the text say," you are now ready to enter the interpretation phase of the inductive method where you will ask the question, "What does the text mean?" As you are studying, ask the question, "What would the text have meant to the original audience?" before you even begin to ask what it should mean for your life. The background information you read will be very helpful in answering this question. Complete the following steps to help you understand the intended meaning of the passage.

1. *Read the text in other versions.* Because the original Hebrew, Aramaic, and Greek of the Bible do not translate perfectly into English, reading different translations of the Bible can help you gain a better understanding of the nuances of the text. Remember that no one translation of the Bible is perfect except the original language. Be careful to use translations of the Bible rather than paraphrases, like The Message, that act as commentaries.
2. *Read cross-references.* Cross-references may take you to other passages of Scripture that speak on the same subject and can provide you with a fuller understanding of that topic. Cross references may also take you to the source of a quotation that an author used from another book of the Bible. Seeing how the same verse appears in more than one part of the Bible gives light to the meaning of both passages. One of the most important hermeneutical principles is that Scripture is the best interpreter of Scripture. The 39 books of the Old Testament and the 27 books of the New Testament are all the Word of God, and therefore all work together without contradiction to tell the story of God's redemption. Cross-references are incredible tools to help you apply this hermeneutical principle in your study time.

3. *Paraphrase or summarize the passage.* You may feel confident in your understanding of a passage only to realize when you try to write it in your own words how much you do not understand. Paraphrasing the text forces us to stop and check for understanding rather than skipping over parts that may be confusing without even realizing that we are doing it. Don't let this step be paralyzing; it is okay if your initial interpretation is wrong. You can always come back and rewrite your paraphrase as your knowledge and understanding of God's Word grows.
4. *Identify how the text reflects the metanarrative of Scripture, which is the story of creation, fall, redemption, and restoration.* All of Scripture is God's story of redemption, and all of Scripture points to the Redeemer, Jesus Christ. When you study a passage, ask yourself how the smaller story you are reading reflects the bigger story that spans across the entire Bible. Ask yourself how Christ is the true and better version of those we see in the pages of Scripture, how the Old Testament prophets anticipate the coming Messiah, and how Jesus is the answer to the needs and problems we see arise in the Word.
5. *Read trustworthy commentaries if you need further insight into the meaning of the passage.* It is important that you do not consult commentaries until after you have worked through the above steps in the comprehension and interpretation phases on your own. The Bible is the only inerrant book, and while commentaries can be extremely helpful, they do not have the same authority as God's Word. We need to practice studying and interpreting the Bible on our own so that we can confidently test other writings against the truth of Scripture.

STEPS FOR PROPER INTERPRETATION

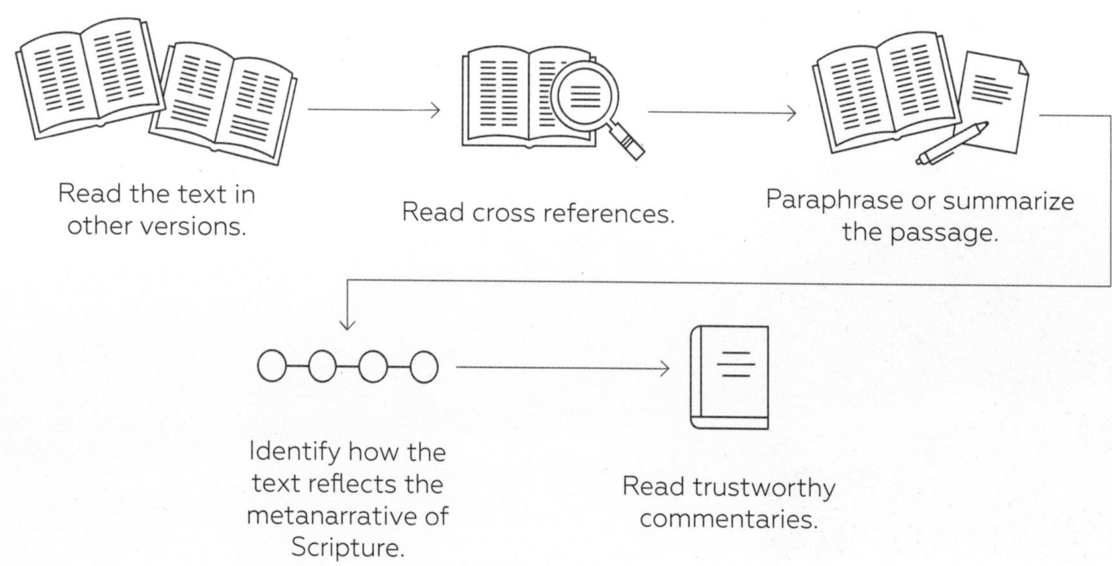

How will the background information you learned from the observation phase help you as you begin the interpretation process?

What is some information that you discovered in the observation phase that will help you in this interpretation phase?

Which of these steps have you taken when interpreting Scripture in the past? Which are new to you?

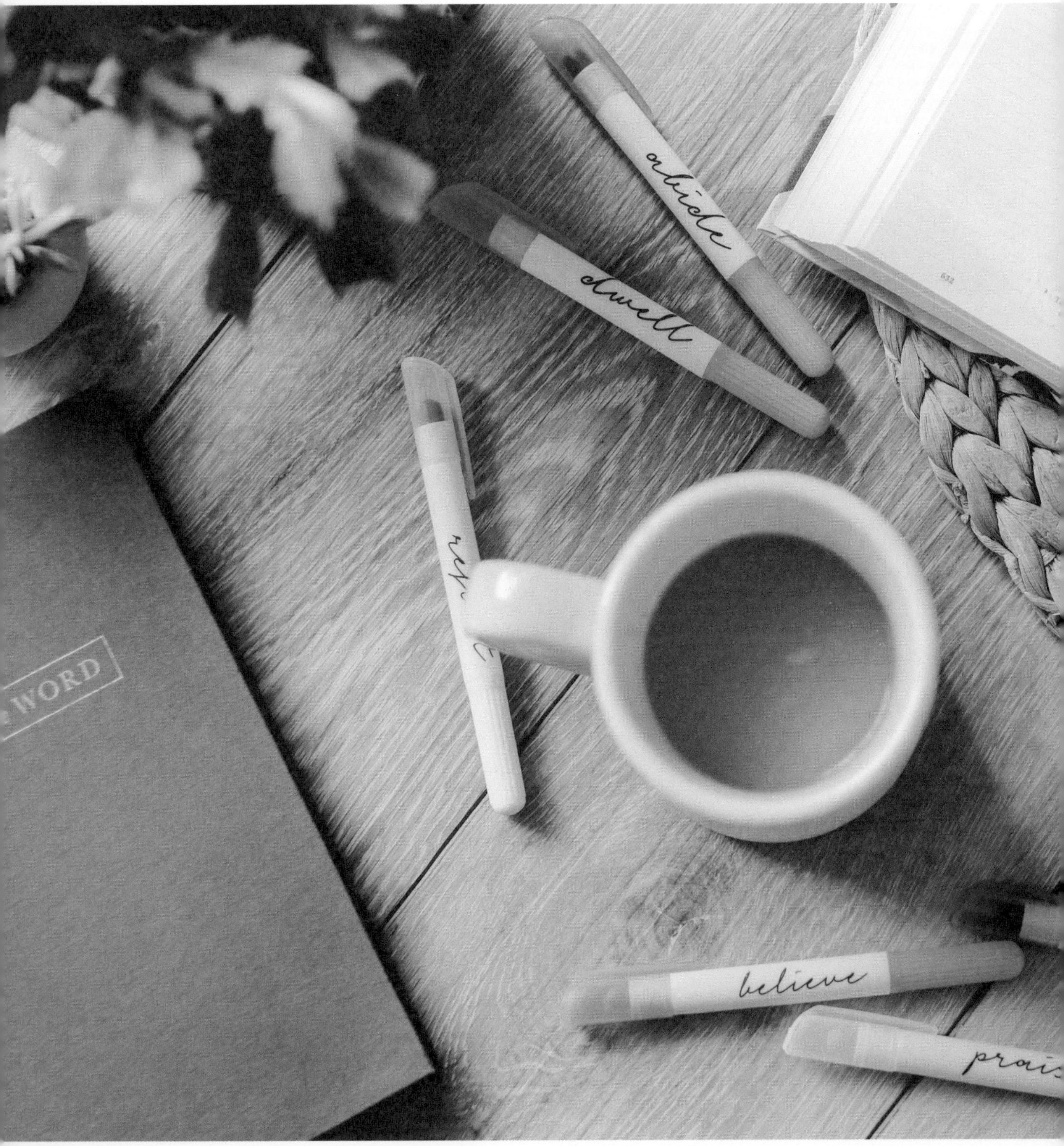
abide
dwell
believe
WORD

ISAIAH 40:8

—

The grass withers, the flowers fade, but the word of our God remains forever.

Reading in Multiple Versions

WORKSHEET GUIDANCE:

In addition to the CSB version that you annotated, read 1 Peter 2:1-12 in three other versions (Suggestions: ESV, NASB, NIV, KJV, NKJV). You can access all of these versions at *www.biblegateway.com.*

Note any differences that give you a better understanding of the text in the chart below before answering the questions that follow.

CSB			

How did reading the passage in different versions help answer any of your questions about the text?

What additional insights did you gain about the text by reading different versions?

Did any of the versions use different words than the CSB where you had noted unfamiliar words? Does the differing word choice help bring light to the meaning of the text?

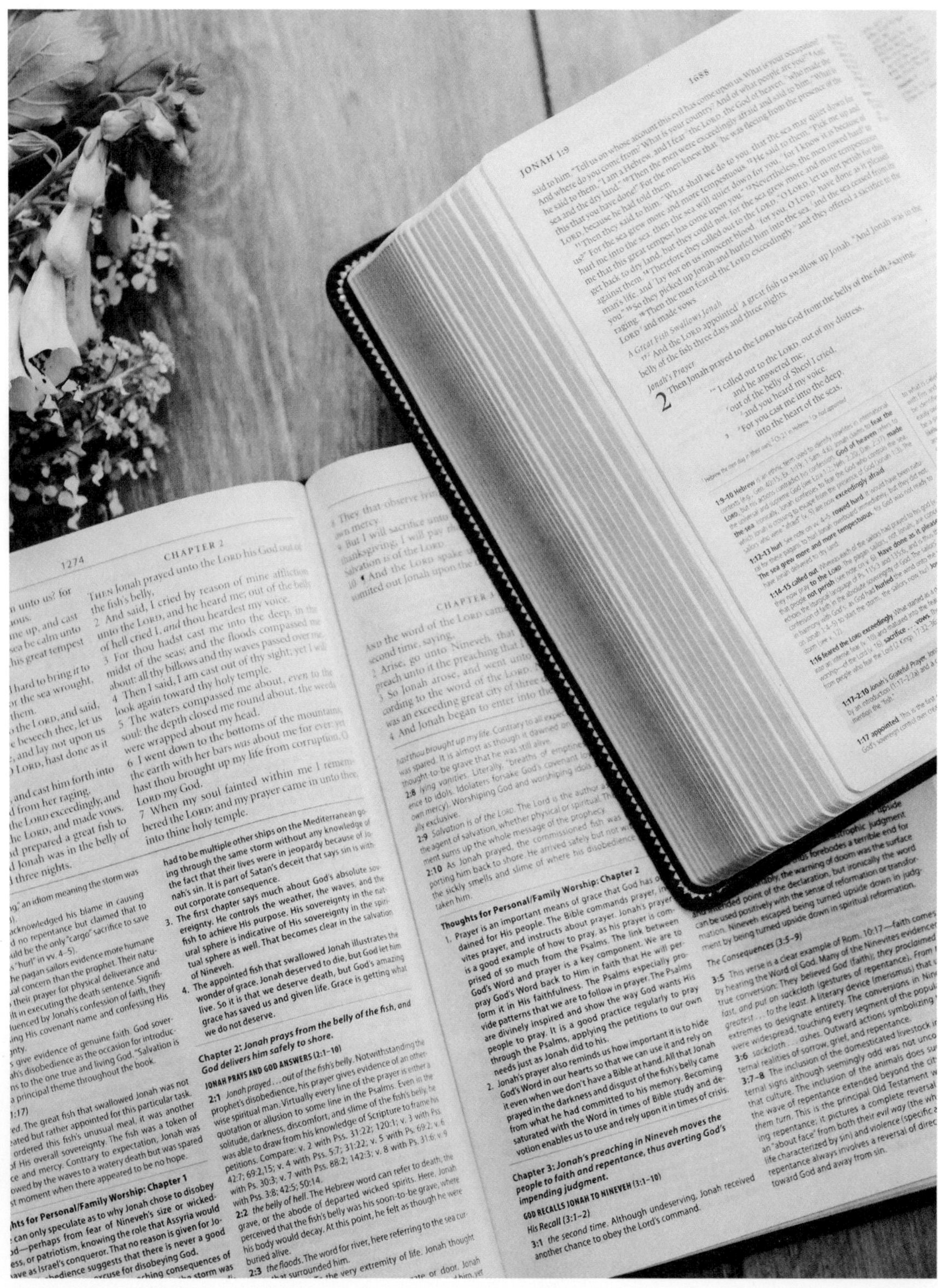
JONAH 1:9
1688
1274
CHAPTER 2

Cross References

Peter directly quotes three Old Testament verses in 1 Peter 2:1-12. As we study the Bible, it is important to remember the principle that "Scripture interprets Scripture," and cross-references are a great tool to help us employ this principle.

WORKSHEET GUIDANCE:

- Read each of the quoted verses from their original sources (Isaiah 28:16, Psalm 118:22, and Isaiah 8:14), as well as the verses that surround them to get an idea of the context in which they occur, then answer the following questions.

How does reading the three Old Testament passages give you a deeper understanding of the passage from 1 Peter?

How does Peter's use of these three verses help you interpret the Old Testament passages? How does it help you see Christ in these Old Testament passages?

Oftentimes biblical authors will indirectly reference another passage of Scripture or allude to an event in the Bible, rather than directly quoting from it. The more we study the Bible, the more we will recognize these uses of Scripture, and cross-references can help point us to those passages even if we do not immediately pick up on them. 1 Peter 2 contains several such uses of Scripture. Answer the questions below based on some of these cross-references.

1 Peter 2:3 references Psalm 34:8. Read Psalm 34:8 and the surrounding verses. Based on this verse, what do you think Peter means when he mentions tasting that the Lord is good?

1 Peter 2:9 employs the language of multiple Old Testament passages to describe his Christian audience. Read the verses listed below, along with the surrounding verses, and use the space provided to answer the questions about each one.

DEUTERONOMY 10:15

What is happening in Deuteronomy 10?

To whom is Moses speaking when he tells them they are God's chosen people?

EXODUS 19:5-6

What is happening in Exodus 19?

Whom does God call His treasured possession, a kingdom of priests, and a holy nation?

The word "therefore" in verse five indicates a reason why God gives these names to His people. What does the "therefore" point back to? See verses 1-4.

When God gave the Israelites the law, He made a covenant with them that established them as God's people. This is a binding covenant. As God's people, they were recipients of the promises that God has made to Abraham, Isaac, and Jacob. What does Peter's use of this covenant language in 1 Peter tell you about what it means to be a Christian?

Some cross references do not indicate an intentional reference by the author to another passage of Scripture, yet they point to other places in the Bible that discuss the same topic. Because all Scripture is the Word of God, reading what different biblical authors have to say about a topic is incredibly valuable for interpreting the meaning behind an individual passage. 1 Peter 2:2 talks about being like a newborn infant and longing for pure spiritual milk. Read the following cross-references and their surrounding verses, and write in the spaces provided how each one impacts your understanding of 1 Peter 2:2.

1 CORINTHIANS 3:2

HEBREWS 5:12-13

1 Peter 2:5 talks about offering spiritual sacrifices to God. Read the following cross-references and their surrounding verses, and write in the spaces provided how each one impacts your understanding of what it means to offer spiritual sacrifices.

ISAIAH 56:7

ROMANS 12:1

HEBREWS 13:15

Paraphrasing

You have worked very closely with 1 Peter 2:1-12, and you likely have a much greater understanding of it than you did after your initial reading. Paraphrasing is a helpful tool to check for comprehension and any remaining gaps in your understanding, as well as a means to engage your brain even more actively as you process through the text at a deeper level. When you paraphrase a text, you are writing it in your own words. Unlike summarizing, whose goal is to recount the major points and overall argument of the text, paraphrasing occurs at the sentence level and is a restating of each individual verse of the text using different words.

WORKSHEET GUIDANCE:

Use the space provided in the pages that follow to write 1 Peter 2:1-12, verse by verse, in your own words. If you come across a portion of the text that you are struggling to rewrite, it might indicate a gap in your understanding. Go back to your annotated text, and re-read it in its context. Consider looking into additional cross-references and reading the text in other versions.

If you still have questions about the text, do your best to paraphrase it, and then write your remaining questions in the space provided at the end of your paraphrase. (Paraphrase tip: write your paraphrase in pencil so that you can come back later and make changes).

QUESTIONS

Finding the Metanarrative

WORKSHEET GUIDANCE:

Read through 1 Peter 2:1-12 again, and use the chart to note how the passage points to the four parts of the metanarrative of Scripture: creation, fall, redemption, and restoration.

Consider these questions when filling out your chart:

CREATION: How does this passage point to God as Creator?
What has God brought into existence in this passage?
How does this passage highlight God's plan?
How does this passage point to God's sustaining work?
How does this passage point to God's sovereignty?

FALL: How does this passage point to man's fallen nature?
What sin does the passage call us to avoid?
How does this passage show the effects of sin?

REDEMPTION: How does this passage point to Christ?
How does the text show the transformation that God works in us?

RESTORATION: How does this passage point to our future hope?

CREATION	FALL	REDEMPTION	RESTORATION

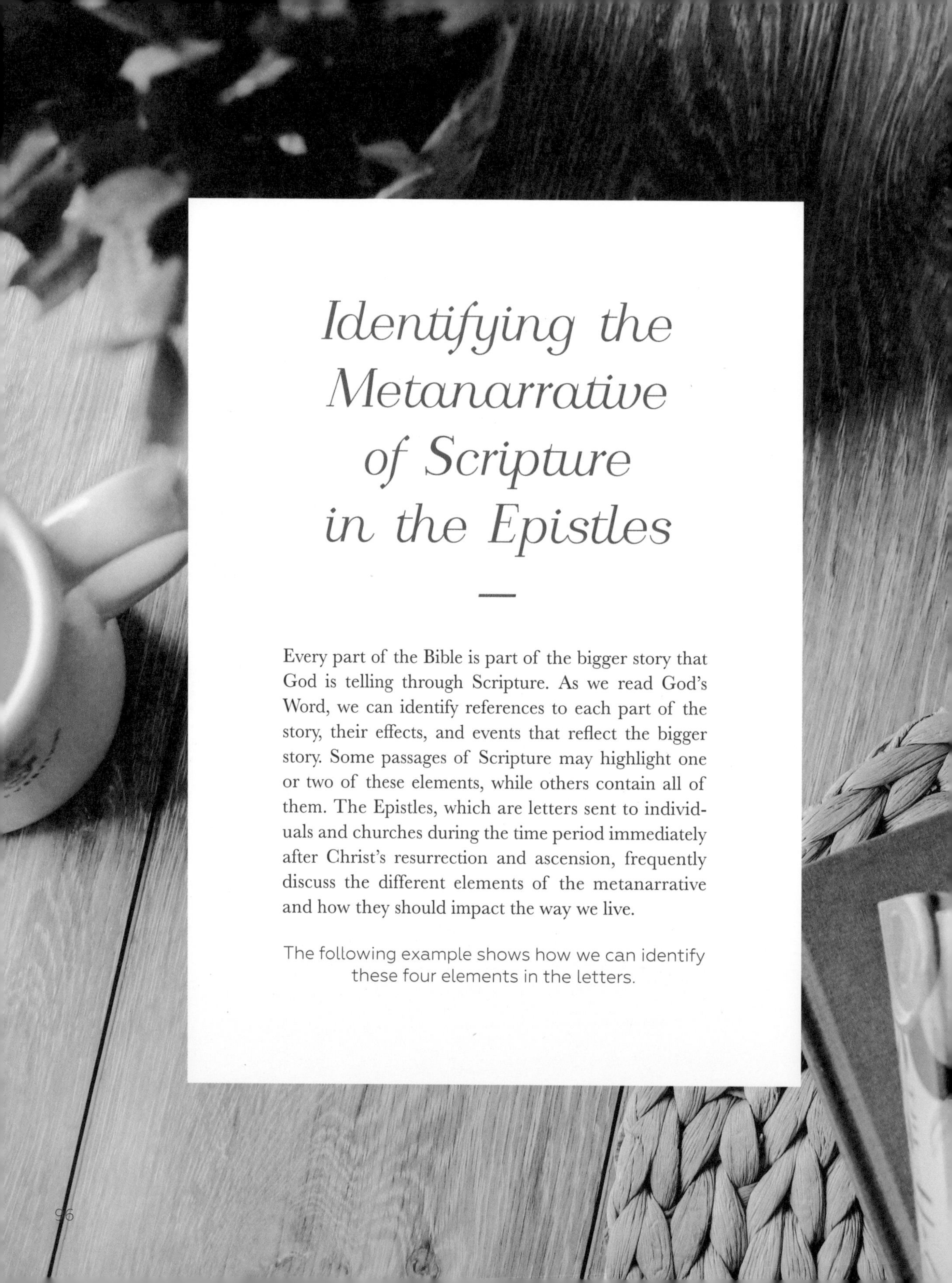

Identifying the Metanarrative of Scripture in the Epistles

Every part of the Bible is part of the bigger story that God is telling through Scripture. As we read God's Word, we can identify references to each part of the story, their effects, and events that reflect the bigger story. Some passages of Scripture may highlight one or two of these elements, while others contain all of them. The Epistles, which are letters sent to individuals and churches during the time period immediately after Christ's resurrection and ascension, frequently discuss the different elements of the metanarrative and how they should impact the way we live.

The following example shows how we can identify these four elements in the letters.

Key: Creation Fall Redemption Restoration

Ephesians 1:3-12

3 Blessed is the God and Father of our Lord Jesus Christ, who has blessed us with every spiritual
blessing in the heavens in Christ. 4 For he chose us in him, before the foundation of the world, to
be holy and blameless in love before him. 5 He predestined us to be adopted as sons through Jesus
Christ for himself, according to the good pleasure of his will, 6 to the praise of his glorious grace
that he lavished on us in the Beloved One.

7 In him we have redemption through his blood, the forgiveness of our trespasses, according to the
riches of his grace 8 that he richly poured out on us with all wisdom and understanding. 9 He made
known to us the mystery of his will, according to his good pleasure that he purposed in Christ
10 as a plan for the right time—to bring everything together in Christ, both things in heaven and
things on earth in him.

11 In him we have also received an inheritance, because we were predestined according to the plan
of the one who works out everything in agreement with the purpose of his will, 12 so that we who
had already put our hope in Christ might bring praise to his glory.

WORKSHEET GUIDANCE:

Underline or highlight the four elements of the metanarrative for the following passage:

Creation: Mark any references to God as Creator.

Fall: Mark anything that indicates our sin nature because of the fall.

Redemption: Mark anything that refers to God's saving work in us.

Restoration: Mark any reference to the future hope we have because of Jesus Christ.

Colossians 1:3-17

3We always thank God, the Father of our Lord Jesus Christ, when we pray for you, 4for we have heard of your faith in Christ Jesus and of the love you have for all the saints 5because of the hope reserved for you in heaven. You have already heard about this hope in the word of truth, the gospel 6that has come to you. It is bearing fruit and growing all over the world, just as it has among you since the day you heard it and came to truly appreciate God's grace. 7You learned this from Epaphras, our dearly loved fellow servant. He is a faithful minister of Christ on your behalf, 8and he has told us about your love in the Spirit.

9For this reason also, since the day we heard this, we haven't stopped praying for you. We are asking that you may be filled with the knowledge of his will in all wisdom and spiritual understanding, 10so that you may walk worthy of the Lord, fully pleasing to him: bearing fruit in every good work and growing in the knowledge of God, 11being strengthened with all power, according to his glorious might, so that you may have great endurance and patience, joyfully 12giving thanks to the Father, who has enabled you to share in the saints' inheritance in the light. 13He has rescued us from the domain of darkness and transferred us into the kingdom of the Son he loves. 14In him we have redemption, the forgiveness of sins.

15He is the image of the invisible God,
the firstborn over all creation.
16For everything was created by him,
in heaven and on earth,
the visible and the invisible,
whether thrones or dominions
or rulers or authorities—
all things have been created through him
and for him.
17He is before all things,
and by him all things hold together.

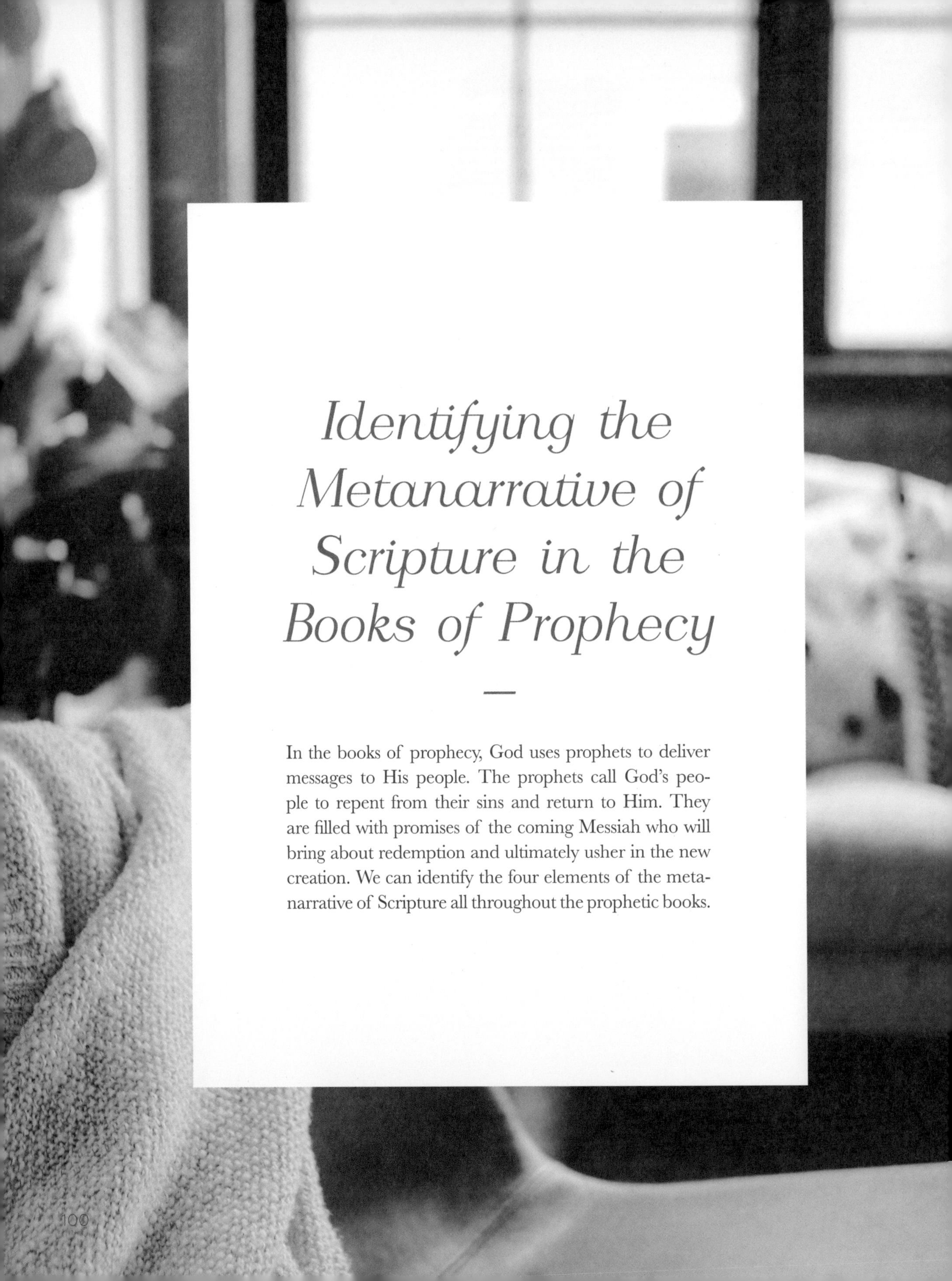

Identifying the Metanarrative of Scripture in the Books of Prophecy

In the books of prophecy, God uses prophets to deliver messages to His people. The prophets call God's people to repent from their sins and return to Him. They are filled with promises of the coming Messiah who will bring about redemption and ultimately usher in the new creation. We can identify the four elements of the metanarrative of Scripture all throughout the prophetic books.

CREATION:

In the prophetic books, God often describes Himself in terms of His creative work.

Look for any references to Him forming people and the world, how humans are made in God's image, or His sovereignty over creation.

FALL:

The books of prophecy specifically highlight the call to repent from sin and the need for a savior, all of which are results of the fall.

Look for any references to the ways that God's people have rebelled against Him, His judgment against sin, and the call to repent.

REDEMPTION:

The prophets are filled with the promised hope of redemption.

Look for any references to God sending a savior or a Messiah, God forgetting or forgiving wrong, God bringing His people back to their land or back to Himself, God purifying His people, etc.

RESTORATION:

The prophets not only look forward to Christ's first coming, but to His second, when He will consummate the kingdom and make all things new.

Look for times when the prophetic books mention a future hope, a new heaven and new earth, a new covenant, references to God dwelling among His people, an everlasting throne or kingdom, etc.

The following examples show how we can identify the four elements of the metanarrative in the books of prophecy:

Key: Creation Fall Redemption Restoration

Jeremiah 3:12b-14

12b"Return, unfaithful Israel.
This is the Lord's declaration.
I will not look on you with anger,
for I am unfailing in my love.
This is the Lord's declaration.
I will not be angry forever.
13Only acknowledge your guilt—
you have rebelled against the
Lord your God.
You have scattered your favors
to strangers
under every green tree
and have not obeyed me.
This is the Lord's declaration.
14Return, you faithless children—this is the
Lord's declaration—for I am your master,
and I will take you, one from a city and two
from a family, and I will bring you to Zion.

Isaiah 65:17-19

17"For I will create a new heaven
and a new earth;
the past events will not be
remembered or come to mind.
18Then be glad and rejoice forever
in what I am creating;
for I will create Jerusalem to be a joy
and its people to be a delight.
19I will rejoice in Jerusalem
and be glad in my people.
The sound of weeping and crying
will no longer be heard in her.

WORKSHEET GUIDANCE:

Underline or highlight the four elements of the Metanarrative for the following passages.

Key: Creation Fall Redemption Restoration

Jeremiah 12:14-17

[14]This is what the Lord says: "Concerning all my evil neighbors who at-
tack the inheritance that I bequeathed to my people, Israel, I am about to
uproot them from their land, and I will uproot the house of Judah from
them. [15]After I have uprooted them, I will once again have compassion
on them and return each one to his inheritance and to his land. [16]If they
will diligently learn the ways of my people—to swear by my name, 'As
the Lord lives,' just as they taught my people to swear by Baal—they will
be built up among my people. [17]However, if they will not obey, then I will
uproot and destroy that nation." This is the Lord's declaration.

Isaiah 43:1-7

1 Now this is what the Lord says—

the one who created you, Jacob,

and the one who formed you, Israel—

"Do not fear, for I have redeemed you;

I have called you by your name; you are mine.

2 I will be with you when you pass through the waters,

and when you pass through the rivers,

they will not overwhelm you.

You will not be scorched

when you walk through the fire,

and the flame will not burn you.

3 For I am the Lord your God,

the Holy One of Israel,

and your Savior.

I have given Egypt as a ransom for you,

Cush and Seba in your place.

4 Because you are precious in my sight
and honored, and I love you,
I will give people in exchange for you
and nations instead of your life.
5 Do not fear, for I am with you;
I will bring your descendants
from the east,
and gather you from the west.
6 I will say to the north, 'Give them up!'
and to the south, 'Do not hold them back!'
Bring my sons from far away,
and my daughters from the ends
of the earth—
7 everyone who bears my name
and is created for my glory.
I have formed them;
indeed, I have made them."

HEBREWS 4:12

—

For the word of God is living and effective and sharper than any double-edged sword, penetrating as far as the separation of soul and spirit, joints and marrow. It is able to judge the thoughts and intentions of the heart.

Identifying the Metanarrative of Scripture in Historical Narrative

—

Much of the Old Testament falls under the category of historical narrative, recounting real events that occurred throughout history. As we read historical narrative in the Bible, it is important to identify where the story falls in the timeline of redemptive history by looking at the historical context of the book. In terms of the metanarrative of Scripture, some passages directly reflect one of the four plot movements, such as Genesis 1-2 describing creation, while Genesis 3 recounts the fall. More often than not, however, identifying how an individual narrative fits into the larger narrative may not be quite so straightforward. Sometimes we can observe how different elements of the metanarrative impact the storylines of the narratives we read. For example, evil behavior in Scripture reminds us of the reality of the fall and our need for redemption. Many narratives serve as insufficient examples of the greater redemption and restoration that is to come. As we approach historical narrative, we should ask ourselves how the text points back to God's creation of the universe and the fall of man and how it points forward to the redemption that would be accomplished in Christ and the restoration that will occur when Christ consummates His kingdom.

The examples on the following pages show how we can identify the metanarrative of Scripture in historical narrative.

Context: The Exodus story is foundational to God's character and redeeming work. The Old Testament frequently refers back to the Exodus as a pivotal moment in God's revelation of who He is and how He is working to redeem His people. God multiplied Abraham's offspring, just as He said He would, and they find themselves oppressed and enslaved in Egypt. God raises up Moses to deliver his people from slavery, and He sends plagues of judgment upon Egypt so that the Pharaoh would let the Israelites go free. In the final plague, God sent a messenger to take the life of every firstborn in Egypt, but He spared the Israelites by instituting the Passover. God's people were to kill a spotless lamb and paint its blood over their door frame so that the angel of death would pass over their household. After this final plague, God delivered His people out of slavery into the wilderness, parting the Red Sea and destroying the Egyptians who pursued the Israelites. Despite Israel's unfaithfulness, God provided for them in the wilderness and eventually brought them into Canaan, the land God had promised Moses. As we consider the metanarrative of Scripture, the Exodus points forward to the redemption that Christ would accomplish, delivering God's people from their slavery to sin, sustaining them, and ultimately bringing them into the true land of promise when He ushers in the new heaven and new earth.

Key: Creation Fall Redemption Restoration

The numerous offspring of Abraham are evidence of God's creative work to bring something from nothing.

Exodus 1:8-12

8A new king, who did not know about Joseph, came to power in Egypt.
9He said to his people, "Look, the Israelite people are more numerous
and powerful than we are. 10Come, let's deal shrewdly with them; otherwise they will multiply further, and when war breaks out, they will join
our enemies, fight against us, and leave the country." 11So the Egyptians
assigned taskmasters over the Israelites to oppress them with forced labor. They built Pithom and Rameses as supply cities for Pharaoh. 12But
the more they oppressed them, the more they multiplied and spread so
that the Egyptians came to dread the Israelites.

Oppression is a result of sin.

God is not only the Creator, but the Sustainer of life.

Exodus 2:23-25

Difficult labor is part of the curse of the fall.

23After a long time, the king of Egypt died. The Israelites groaned because of their difficult labor; and they cried out; and their cry for help
because of the difficult labor ascended to God. 24And God heard their
groaning; and God remembered his covenant with Abraham, with Isaac,
and with Jacob; 25and God saw the Israelites; and God knew.

God's covenant with Abraham is part of His promise to redeem a people for Himself.

All suffering and injustice is a result of sin.

Exodus 3:7-8

7Then the Lord said, "I have observed the misery of my people in Egypt,
and have heard them crying out because of their oppressors. I know
about their sufferings, 8and I have come down to rescue them from the
power of the Egyptians and to bring them from that land to a good and
spacious land, a land flowing with milk and honey—the territory of the
Canaanites, Hethites, Amorites, Perizzites, Hivites, and Jebusites."

God redeemed the Israelites out of slavery when He rescued them, which is a picture of redemption in Christ.

While God brings the Israelites into the physical land of Canaan, He will ultimately bring His people into the true promised land, the new Heaven and new earth, when Christ returns.

Sin, which is a result of the fall, always merits judgment.

Exodus 12:12-13

12"I will pass through the land of Egypt on that night and strike every
firstborn male in the land of Egypt, both people and animals. I am the
Lord; I will execute judgments against all the gods of Egypt. 13The blood
on the houses where you are staying will be a distinguishing mark for
you; when I see the blood, I will pass over you. No plague will be among
you to destroy you when I strike the land of Egypt.

God offers salvation to His people through the sacrifice of another. The spotless Passover Lamb points forward to Jesus Christ, the Lamb of God, who would accomplish our redemption through His blood.

God brings just judgment upon sin, which is a result of the fall.

Exodus 12:29-32

29 Now at midnight the Lord struck every firstborn male in the land of Egypt, from the firstborn of Pharaoh who sat on his throne to the firstborn of the prisoner who was in the dungeon, and every firstborn of the livestock. 30 During the night Pharaoh got up, he along with all his officials and all the Egyptians, and there was a loud wailing throughout Egypt because there wasn't a house without someone dead. 31 He summoned Moses and Aaron during the night and said, "Get out immediately from among my people, both you and the Israelites, and go, worship the Lord as you have said. 32 Take even your flocks and your herds as you asked and leave, and also bless me."

The Israelites were sinful and deserving of death, but God offered a way for them to escape judgment.

Exodus 14:10-14

10 As Pharaoh approached, the Israelites looked up and there were the
Egyptians coming after them! The Israelites were terrified and cried out
to the Lord for help. 11 They said to Moses: "Is it because there are no
graves in Egypt that you have taken us away to die in the wilderness?
What have you done to us by bringing us out of Egypt? 12 Isn't this what
we told you in Egypt: Leave us alone so that we may serve the Egyptians?
It would have been better for us to serve the Egyptians than to die in the
wilderness." 13 But Moses said to the people, "Don't be afraid. Stand firm
and see the Lord's salvation that he will accomplish for you today; for the
Egyptians you see today, you will never see again. The Lord will fight for
you, and you must be quiet."

Just as God saves the Israelites, He saves all who put their faith in Christ.

Exodus 14:21-22

21 Then Moses stretched out his hand over the sea. The Lord drove the
sea back with a powerful east wind all that night and turned the sea into
dry land. So the waters were divided, 22 and the Israelites went through
the sea on dry ground, with the waters like a wall to them on their right
and their left.

By parting the Red Sea, God offered a way for Israel to be saved from destruction, and He offers a way for all believers to escape death through Christ.

WORKSHEET GUIDANCE:

Read the book of Ruth, and note places where you see the four elements of the metanarrative reflected.

Context: The book of Ruth gives a picture of the redemption that believers have in Jesus Christ. The book takes place during the time of the Judges. After God delivered the Israelite's into the Promised Land, they rebelled against Him, living in sin and turning to other gods. Throughout this time period, God sent judgment upon Israel to cause the people to repent and return to Him, followed by judges to rescue them. The story of Ruth is one of hope and redemption in the midst of a very dark period of time. In this book, an Israelite woman named Naomi and her family flee to the land of Moab, one of Israel's enemies, to escape a famine. While there, her husband dies, and her two sons marry Moabite women, Ruth and Orpah. Her sons die as well, leaving Naomi and her daughters-in-law in an incredibly vulnerable state. Naomi returns home, and while Orpah agrees to go back to her family, Ruth remains loyal to Naomi and goes with her. In Israel, Ruth seeks to glean in a barley field to provide food for Naomi and herself, and she ends up in the field of Boaz, who turns out to be a relative of her late father-in-law. Boaz takes notice of her and blesses her abundantly for her loyalty to Naomi and her willingness to serve the one true God of Israel. Ruth approaches Boaz and requests that He redeem her and Naomi's family line by marrying her. Boaz is willing and able to marry Ruth, redeeming her broken family and restoring Naomi's family line. The book concludes with the genealogy of Ruth's son by Boaz, ending with David, from whom Jesus Christ would come.

CREATION	FALL	REDEMPTION	RESTORATION

RESTING
ON GOD
O God Most High, Most Glorious,

Using Commentaries

After working through the previous steps of the comprehension and interpretation phases, you will likely find that many of the questions you had along the way have been resolved. However, there are probably still parts of the text that you find difficult to understand. If you have carefully worked through the text and still need more information, consulting reliable commentaries can be very helpful. Oftentimes our confusion is due to a missing piece of historical or cultural information or a language barrier due to translation of the original language into English. A great place to start is the notes of a study Bible, such as the ESV Study Bible. This built-in commentary may be enough to answer your question, but if not, you can consult more in-depth commentaries from reputable biblical scholars. The Daily Grace Co. offers a study on the book of 1 Peter called *Grace in the Wilderness* that includes accessible commentary on the entire book. If you are unsure what commentaries to use, consider reaching out to a pastor or trusted Christian mentor to ask for commentary recommendations, or visit websites like *bestcommentaries.com* to read reviews on commentaries for each book of the Bible.

WORKSHEET GUIDANCE:

Go back to the questions you noted at the end of your paraphrase (page 91). Consult a study Bible or other reliable commentaries, and write any answers you found to your remaining questions in the space provided.

gentleness
goodness
patience
joy
kindness
peace

Summarizing

WORKSHEET GUIDANCE:

You have done the hard work of engaging with the text in order to understand its meaning. In the space below write a summary of 1 Peter 2:1-12. While your paraphrase was a verse by verse re-wording of the text, your summary should be a shorter explanation of the main points of the text.

Attributes of God

Eternal

God has no beginning and no end. He always was, always is, and always will be.

HAB. 1:12 / REV. 1:8 / IS. 41:4

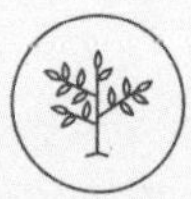

Faithful

God is incapable of anything but fidelity. He is loyally devoted to His plan and purpose.

2 TIM. 2:13 / DEUT. 7:9 / HEB. 10:23

Glorious

God is ultimately beautiful, deserving of all praise and honor.

REV. 19:1 / PS. 104:1
EX. 40:34-35

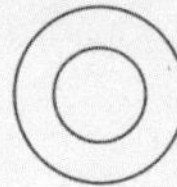

Good

God is pure; there is no defilement in Him. He is unable to sin, and all He does is good.

GEN. 1:31 / PS. 34:8 / PS. 107:1

Gracious

God is kind, giving to us gifts and benefits which we are undeserving of.

2 KINGS 13:23 / PS. 145:8
IS. 30:18

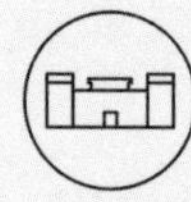

Holy

God is undefiled and unable to be in the presence of defilement. He is sacred and set-apart.

REV. 4:8 / LEV. 19:2 / HAB. 1:13

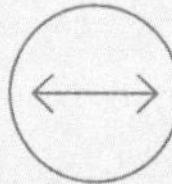

Immutable

God does not change. He is the same yesterday, today, and tomorrow.

1 SAM. 15:29 / ROM. 11:29
JAMES 1:17

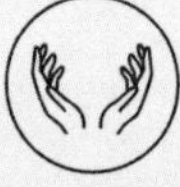

Jealous

God is desirous of receiving the praise and affection He rightly deserves.

EX. 20:5 / DEUT. 4:23-24
JOSH. 24:19

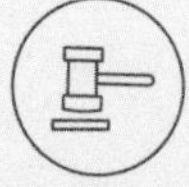

Just

God governs in perfect justice. He acts in accordance with justice. In Him there is no wrongdoing or dishonesty.

IS. 61:8 / DEUT. 32:4 / PS. 146:7-9

Love

God is eternally, enduringly, steadfastly loving and affectionate. He does not forsake or betray His covenant love.

JN. 3:16 / EPH. 2:4-5 / 1 JN. 4:16

Merciful

God is compassionate, withholding us from the wrath that we are deserving of.

TITUS 3:5 / PS. 25:10 / LAM. 3:22-23

Omnipotent

God is all-powerful; His strength is unlimited.

MAT. 19:26 / JOB 42:1-2
JER. 32:27

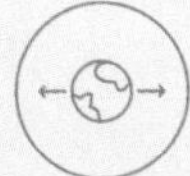

Omnipresent

God is everywhere; His presence is near and permeating.

PROV. 15:3 / PS. 139:7-10
JER. 23:23-24

Omniscient

God is all-knowing; there is nothing unknown to Him.

PS. 147:4 / I JN. 3:20 / HEB. 4:13

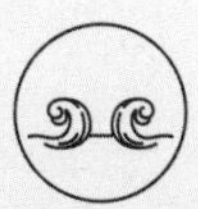

Patient

God is long-suffering and enduring. He gives amply opportunity for people to turn toward Him.

ROM. 2:4 / 2 PET. 3:9 / PS. 86:15

Righteous

God is blameless and upright. There is no wrong found in Him.

PS. 119:137 / JER. 12:1 / REV. 15:3

Sovereign

God governs over all things; He is in complete control.

COL. 1:17 / PS. 24:1-2
1 CHRON. 29:11-12

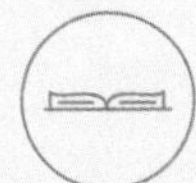

True

God is our measurement of what is fact. By Him are we able to discern true and false.

JN. 3:33 / ROM. 1:25 / JN. 14:6

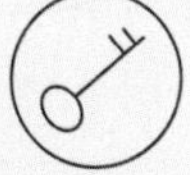

Wise

God is infinitely knowledgeable and is judicious with His knowledge.

IS. 46:9-10 / IS. 55:9 / PROV. 3:19

Ask the question, "How should the truth of this passage change me?"

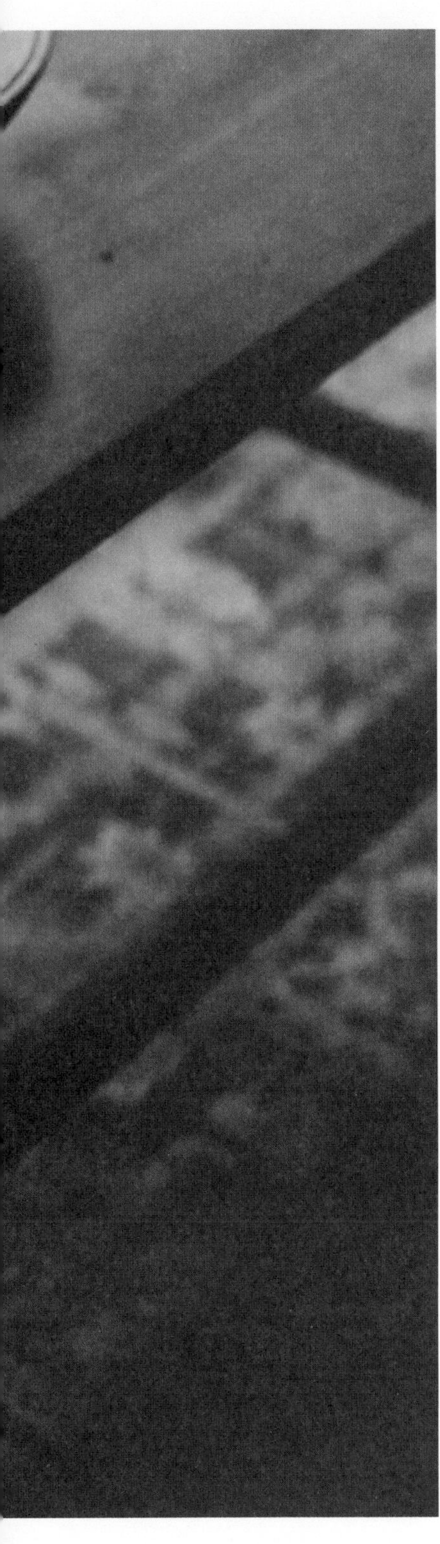

Application

We have come to the final phase of the inductive method, which is the Application phase. Once we have worked to gain a better understanding of what the text says and what it means, we are ready to ask the question, "How should the truth of this passage change me?" Although our tendency is to quickly jump to this step, it is only after we have done the hard work of comprehension and interpretation to see who God has revealed Himself to be in the text that we can then see our own need for His transforming grace in light of that truth. Based on the information you gathered from the previous steps, answer the following questions:

1. *What attributes of God's character are revealed in the passage?* Look for places where the author directly states the character of God, as well as for ways that God reveals His character through His actions. Because God never changes, the truth about God in the Bible is just as true for us today as it was for the original audience. In the Old Testament when God describes Himself as merciful, slow to anger, and abounding in steadfast love, we can know that He is the same—He is still merciful, still slow to anger, and still abounding in steadfast love, and He will forever be so. When we see a God who delivers His people, Israel, out of slavery in Egypt, we can have confidence that the same God delivers us from the bonds of sin.
2. *What do I learn about myself in light of who God is?* When we behold God for who He is, we can see more clearly who we are in relation to His holiness. When we see God's righteousness, love, and grace, we become painfully aware of our own sin, selfishness, and judgmental hearts. Like Isaiah, who upon seeing a vision of the Lord on His throne responds by saying, "Woe is me! For I am lost; for I am a man of unclean lips," so we, too, are humbled by our depravity in contrast to a glimpse of God and cry out, "Holy, holy, holy" (Isaiah 6).

Focusing on our own fallen nature may seem negative or depressing, but in the midst of the devastating news of our sin, the light of the gospel shines through. It is not until we realize the ugliness of our sin and our need for a savior that we can rejoice in the beauty of God's grace to forgive us. If we try to build ourselves up with the message that we possess goodness and strength on our own, we will find ourselves discontent and distanced from God's love, believing that we deserve His forgiveness. But when we realize that we have earned nothing but His wrath, we can stand in awe of the depth of God's love for sinners like us, a love great enough to send His own perfect Son to die that we might live.

3. *How should this truth change me?* The good news is that God does not leave us in our sin, but He graciously works in us, sanctifying us and transforming us into his glorious image. A passage of Scripture may contain direct commands telling us what to do or warnings about sins to avoid in order to help us grow in holiness. Other times our application flows out of seeing ourselves in light of God's character. As we pray and reflect on how God is calling us to change in light of His Word, we should be asking questions like, "How should I pray for God to change my heart?" and "What practical steps can I take toward cultivating habits of holiness?"

James 1:22 calls us to be not just hearers of the Word but also doers of the Word. Our works do not save us, but good works are a result of true saving faith. Let us joyfully seek to be holy as God is holy in the freedom that comes from the knowledge that it is Christ alone who accomplishes our salvation.

QUESTIONS FOR APPLICATION

What attributes of God's character are revealed in the passage? → What do I learn about myself in light of who God is? → How should this truth change me?

How have you approached applying Scripture in the past?

Why is it important to have application as the last step of your study?

God & Man

WORKSHEET GUIDANCE:

The first step to applying a passage of Scripture is recognizing the character of God that the text reveals.

1. Return to your annotated text of 1 Peter 2:1-12 on page 71, and mark or highlight in yellow every place where God's character is directly stated, then list out these character qualities in the first column on the chart below.
2. Go back to the text again, and put a star next to everything that God does in the passage, then write out His actions in the second column of the chart at the bottom of the page and what each action reveals about what God is like in the third column.

GOD'S STATED CHARACTER	GOD'S ACTIONS	GOD'S IMPLIED CHARACTER

3. Based on the information in your chart, write a paragraph describing God as revealed in 1 Peter 2:1-12.

The primary subject of God's Word is God's character, but it also reveals a lot about who we are as well. The biblical authors can reveal information about humanity either directly or indirectly.

1. Look back at each of the characteristics of God listed in the first and last columns of your chart. For each character quality, write in the space below what it reveals about us in relationship to Him (examples: God's holiness reveals our sinfulness; God's patience shows how impatient we can be).

2. Oftentimes Scripture directly describes our sinful nature by pointing out our sins or commanding us not to do something that we have a tendency to do. Go back through the annotated text, and mark or highlight in orange every time the text directly states some kind of sinful quality or behavior.

3. When we see ourselves in relation to God, we see our own sinful nature and the ways that our sinful flesh continues to battle with the redeemed new self. However, for the believer, God's Word also reveals who we are in Christ because of our union with Him. Go back to the text, and highlight in blue everything that is true of us because of our redemption in Christ.

4. Based on your answers to the previous questions, fill out the table below.

OUR SINFUL NATURE	WHO WE ARE IN CHRIST

Life Application

The knowledge of who God is and who we are in relationship to Him should change the way that we live. The good news of the gospel is that it impacts every area of our lives, from the mundane to the monumental.

1. Look back on God's character from the table on the previous page. What should be your response to the qualities that He embodies?

2. Look back on our sinful nature from the previous table. How specifically do you see these sinful tendencies play out in your own life?

3. Write a prayer of confession to God for the sin you recognize in your own life.

4. Look back at who we are in Christ from yesterday's table. How should you live in response to the redemptive work Christ has done in you?

5. Go back to your annotated text on page 71, and think about the commands highlighted in green. What would it look like to put these commands into practice in your own life?

6. What are some specific ways you should live differently in light of who God is and who you are in relationship to Him?

7. What are some specific action steps you can take this week to work toward those changes?

Application Questions

When you reach the application stage of your study, consider asking yourself some of these questions.

IS THERE A TRUTH ABOUT GOD I NEED TO REMEMBER IN THIS PASSAGE?

IS THERE A SIN TO FLEE IN THIS PASSAGE?

IS THERE A COMMAND TO OBEY IN THIS PASSAGE?

IS THERE AN ACTION OR ATTITUDE TO EMULATE IN THIS PASSAGE?

IS THERE A PRINCIPLE TO FOLLOW IN THIS PASSAGE?

IS THERE SOMETHING I NEED TO PRAY?

WHAT DOES THIS PASSAGE REVEAL ABOUT GOD AND HIS CHARACTER?

HOW DOES THIS TEXT REMIND ME OF MY FALLEN CONDITION?

HOW SHOULD THE TRUTH OF WHO GOD IS AS REVEALED IN THIS PASSAGE CHANGE THE WAY I LIVE?

HOW CAN I RESPOND IN LIGHT OF THE REDEMPTION I HAVE BEEN GIVEN?

HOW SHOULD WHAT I HAVE LEARNED ABOUT GOD CHANGE MY HEART AND ATTITUDE TOWARD MY CIRCUMSTANCES?

WHAT PRACTICAL THINGS CAN I DO IN LIGHT OF THIS PASSAGE?

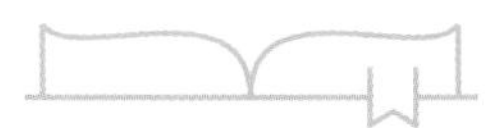

Scripture Memory

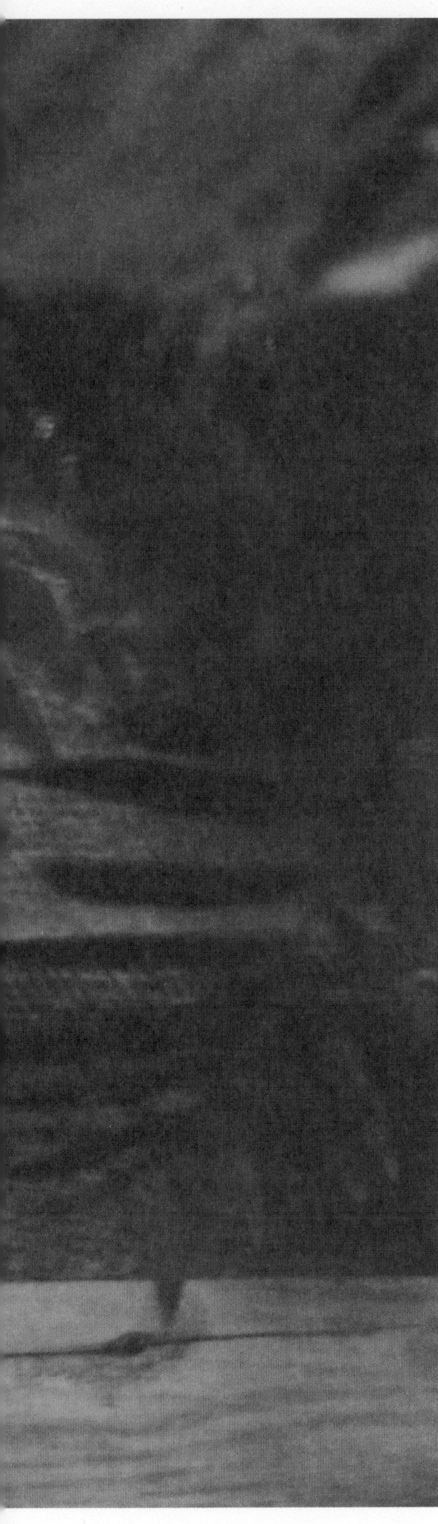

PSALM 119:105

—

Your word is a lamp for my feet and a light on my path.

Christ
et you.
THE LETTER OF PAUL TO THE
COLOSSIANS
Greeting
1 Paul, an apostle of Christ Jesus by the will of God, and Timothy our brother,
2 To the saints and faithful brothers in Christ at Colossae:
Grace to you and peace from God our Father.
Thanksgiving and Prayer
3 We always thank God, the Father of our Lord Jesus Christ, when we pray for
you, 4 since we heard of your faith in Christ Jesus and of the love that you have for
all the saints, 5 because of the hope laid up for you in heaven. Of this you have heard
before in the word of the truth, the gospel, 6 which has come to you, as indeed in
the whole world it is bearing fruit and increasing—as it also does among you,
since the day you heard it and understood the grace of God in truth, 7 just as you
learned it from Epaphras our beloved fellow servant. He is a faithful minister of
Christ on your behalf 8 and has made known to us your love in the Spirit.
9 And so, from the day we heard, we have not ceased to pray for you, asking
that you may be filled with the knowledge of his will in all spiritual wisdom and

WEEK 6

Going Deeper

KNOWING & LOVING GOD

"
God speaks to us through His Word, and we respond to Him in prayer.

Reading:
Psalm 107:31,
1 John 1:9,
Philippians 4:6,
2 Timothy 2:1

Praying Scripture

God speaks to us through His Word, and we respond to Him in prayer. Studying God's Word should not be merely an intellectual exercise but a practice that engages both our heads and our hearts. Therefore, our study of Scripture should always be saturated in prayer from start to finish, and we should respond to what God has revealed to us by praying to Him.

We have focused a lot of our attention in this study on seeking to find how God has revealed Himself in the Bible, and the first thing we should do when we pray in response to His Word is to adore Him for who He is and thank Him for what He has done. Recount His good character and His holy works, and praise Him for those things. As we turn to God in adoration, our desires and delights are shaped to match His.

God's Word also exposes our sin, and we should come to Him in repentance, pleading with Him to purify us. Has God revealed sin in your own heart and life? Pray for forgiveness from those things, and ask Him to empower you to flee from them. Has the text you read given you a command to follow? Ask God to give you the strength to follow it. Have you seen evidence of persistent sin in your life? Ask God to do the transforming work in your heart that only He can do.

Not only can we pray in response to God's Word, but we can also pray the very words of Scripture back to God. Many parts of Scripture contain prayers that we can pray directly. The book of Psalms is saturated with prayers of rejoicing, praise, and lament, and they give words to what we often cannot express on our own. The Epistles contain prayers for God's people to grow in His likeness. Even parts of Scripture that are not explicitly written as prayers can serve to give words to our petitions.

Praying Scripture

WORKSHEET GUIDANCE:

Write a prayer in response to what you have studied in 1 Peter. Look back on your annotated text, as well as the tables you completed about God's character and our sinfulness, to assist you in writing your prayer. As you pray, incorporate some of the language of the text. You can craft your prayer using the following prompts:

Adoration & Thanksgiving: Praise God for who He is and what He has done.

Confession: Confess the sins that the Spirit has exposed in your own life through your study of 1 Peter and ask for forgiveness. Ask God to help you put those sins to death.

Supplication: Ask God to help you follow the commands He has given in this passage. Ask Him to transform your heart. Pray the truths of Scripture for others who come to mind and for the church as a whole.

From Genesis to Revelation, all of Scripture points to Christ.

Christ in All of Scripture: Promises & Prophecy

From Genesis to Revelation, all of Scripture points to Christ. The Old Testament highlights the need for a Savior and anticipates His coming, and the New Testament announces His arrival. We can find Jesus in every book of the Bible, but first we have to learn how to look for Him.

One way that the Bible points to Christ is through prophecies and promises. Many parts of Scripture contain explicit messianic prophecies that predict the coming of Jesus Christ. Many promises and prophecies have an immediate and partial historical fulfillment but a complete fulfillment in Jesus Christ. For example, when God promised to bring the Israelites into the Promised Land, they saw partial fulfillment as Joshua led them across the Jordan river, but we still await the final fulfillment in Jesus Christ, when we who have faith in Him will enter into the true promised land, the new creation, at His second coming.

Many times, a New Testament passage will reference an Old Testament promise or prophecy and explain how it finds its fulfillment in Christ, which is another reason for cross-references that may point you to such passages.

WORKSHEET GUIDANCE:

Isaiah 53 is perhaps the most well-known Old Testament messianic prophecy. Read Isaiah 53, and then use the table below to write details of the prophecy on the left and how they are fulfilled in Christ on the right. To aid you in seeing how Christ fulfills the prophecies in this passage, consider what you know about the gospel from this study, what you have read in Scripture here or on your own, and consider reading the narrative of the Passion found in Matthew 26-28, Mark 14-15, Luke 22-23, and John 18-19.

ISAIAH 53 PROPHECY	FULFILLMENT IN CHRIST

Isaiah 53

1 Who has believed what we have heard?
And to whom has the arm of the
Lord been revealed?

2 He grew up before him like a young plant
and like a root out of dry ground.
He didn't have an impressive form
or majesty that we should look at him,
no appearance that we should desire him.

3 He was despised and rejected by men,
a man of suffering who knew what
sickness was.
He was like someone people turned
away from;
he was despised, and we didn't value him.

4 Yet he himself bore our sicknesses,
and he carried our pains;
but we in turn regarded him stricken,
struck down by God, and afflicted.

5 But he was pierced because of our rebellion,
crushed because of our iniquities;
punishment for our peace was on him,
and we are healed by his wounds.

6 We all went astray like sheep;
we all have turned to our own way;
and the Lord has punished him
for the iniquity of us all.

7 He was oppressed and afflicted,
yet he did not open his mouth.
Like a lamb led to the slaughter
and like a sheep silent before
her shearers,
he did not open his mouth.

8 He was taken away because of
oppression and judgment,
and who considered his fate?
For he was cut off from the land
of the living;
he was struck because of my
people's rebellion.

9 He was assigned a grave with
the wicked,
but he was with a rich man at his death,
because he had done no violence
and had not spoken deceitfully.

10 Yet the Lord was pleased to crush
him severely.
When you make him a guilt offering,
he will see his seed, he will prolong
his days,
and by his hand, the Lord's pleasure
will be accomplished.

11 After his anguish,
he will see light and be satisfied.
By his knowledge,
my righteous servant will justify many,
and he will carry their iniquities.

12 Therefore I will give him the many
as a portion,
and he will receive the mighty as spoil,
because he willingly submitted to death,
and was counted among the rebels;
yet he bore the sin of many
and interceded for the rebels.

Christ in All of Scripture: Need for Christ

One way that Scripture points to Christ is by highlighting the need for Him. Every problem, every bit of pain and suffering we experience, stems from the fall in Genesis 3, and the solution is Jesus Christ. When you read a passage of Scripture, ask yourself the following question: What is the problem presented in this passage? How is Jesus the solution? What is the need presented in this passage? How does Jesus fill it? How does this passage highlight sin? How does Jesus respond?

WORKSHEET GUIDANCE:

Complete the table below by first reading each of the passages of Scripture and writing in the second column the problem, need, or sin that the passage presents. Then, in the third column, record how Jesus responds to those problems.

PASSAGE	PROBLEM, NEED, OR SIN	JESUS AS THE SOLUTION
Genesis 3:8-19		
Psalm 14:1-3		
Isaiah 59:14-20		
Romans 7:15-25		
Galatians 5:19-24		

Christ in All of Scripture: Typology

—

In the Old Testament, one of the major ways that Scripture points to Christ is through biblical typology. Typology is a kind of analogy comparing two things in such a way that the former is an insufficient representation of the latter. In the Bible, there are many types of Christ. A type of Christ is a person, an object, an institution, etc. that serves as a shadow that points forward to the true substance. A type will have similarities and differences to Christ and will point forward to Him as the true and better fulfillment of the thing that partially images Him.

One of the most prominent examples of a type of Christ is King David. When Israel demanded a human king out of their sinful desire to be like other nations, God gave them Saul, a king who ruled wickedly. In response to Saul's sin, God anointed a new king, David, a shepherd who worked out in the fields. David was called a man after God's own heart, and he ruled the people according to God's commands. God made a covenant with David, promising him that his throne would go on forever, and that a king who comes from His line would rule eternally in perfect righteousness and peace in a land where God's people would live in His presence.

David is a type of Christ that finds its fulfillment in Jesus, and David and Jesus have many similarities but also many differences. David was a shepherd over sheep, but Jesus would be a shepherd over God's people. David ruled on a throne for his short lifetime, but Jesus will rule on a throne eternally. David was a man after God's own heart, but he still fell into sin. Jesus is the Son of God who is completely without sin. David rules over Israel, but Christ will rule over the true Israel that includes people from every tribe, tongue, and nation who put their faith in Him. These are just a few of the many comparisons that can be drawn between the two. When we see a type of Christ, we see a glimpse of the hope that Christ will bring, and the insufficiency of the type makes us long for the fulfillment in Jesus Christ.

WORKSHEET GUIDANCE:

Read: Genesis 3, Romans 5:12-21

One type of Christ that the New Testament explicitly mentions is Adam. Using the readings listed above, complete the table below with the comparisons you draw between the type, Adam, and the antitype, Christ. Be sure to include both similarities and differences.

ADAM	CHRIST

How do Adam's shortcomings stir a desire for the second Adam, Jesus Christ?

Theology is the study of who God is...

Biblical Theology Themes

The more you study Scripture, the greater sense you will have of how it all fits together as part of one grand narrative. Biblical theology is an area of study that highlights much of the coherence within the Bible, and an understanding of biblical theology can greatly enhance your understanding of how God reveals Himself in Scripture.

Theology is the study of who God is and what He has revealed in His Word. There are two major approaches to studying theology from Scripture. One approach is called systematic theology, which systematizes the study of God by dividing it into categories and pulling passages from the entire Bible that speak to that topic. Categories of systematic theology include Christology (the study of Christ), Soteriology (the study of Salvation), and Eschatology (the study of the end times), among others. Another approach called biblical theology traces themes that develop chronologically through Scripture. God reveals Himself to us through history and through His Word through progressive revelation, bit by bit, so that the scope of our understanding of God's work of redemption broadens throughout time as recorded in Scripture. Biblical theology traces themes, such as covenants, the dwelling place of God, and worship, as they progressively develop throughout the story of Scripture.

WORKSHEET GUIDANCE:

One major biblical theology theme that develops throughout Scripture is the dwelling place of God.

Read the following passages of Scripture, and fill in details about the different phases of this theme's progression using the graphic on the next page. Then, answer the question below.

Scripture to Use:

Genesis 2-3

Exodus 40:16-38

2 Samuel 7:1-17

1 Kings 6

2 Chronicles 7:1-10

Matthew 1:18-23

John 1:1-18

Ephesians 2:11-22

Revelation 21:1-4

In your own words, explain how the theme of God's dwelling place develops throughout Scripture.

EDEN

THE FALL

TABERNACLE

THE TEMPLE

INCARNATION

BELIEVERS

NEW CREATION

The Interpretation Process

—

This graphic illustrates the proper sequence of interpretation of a passage of Scripture. The solid lines indicate the correct order that protects against misinterpretation, while the dotted lines show the negative outcome of leaving out steps in the process.

1 Interpretation must begin by moving from the text to the original audience. Through exegesis, which is the process of drawing out the intended meaning of the text, we must begin by uncovering what the text would have meant to the original audience in their original context.

2 The next step is to move from the original audience and context to the cross. We should look to determine how the passage is connected to the gospel and how it points to Christ.

3 The final step of the interpretation process is to make the connection from the cross to our current context. In this step, we draw application from the text that retains the original meaning and is rooted in the gospel.

X When we move directly from the text to the cross, we run the risk of allegorizing a text that is not meant to function as an allegory. When we skip the cross and move directly from the original audience to ourselves, the result is a moralistic interpretation of Scripture. If we move directly from the text to our contemporary context, we can end up with allegorical moralism, which is also called contextualization.

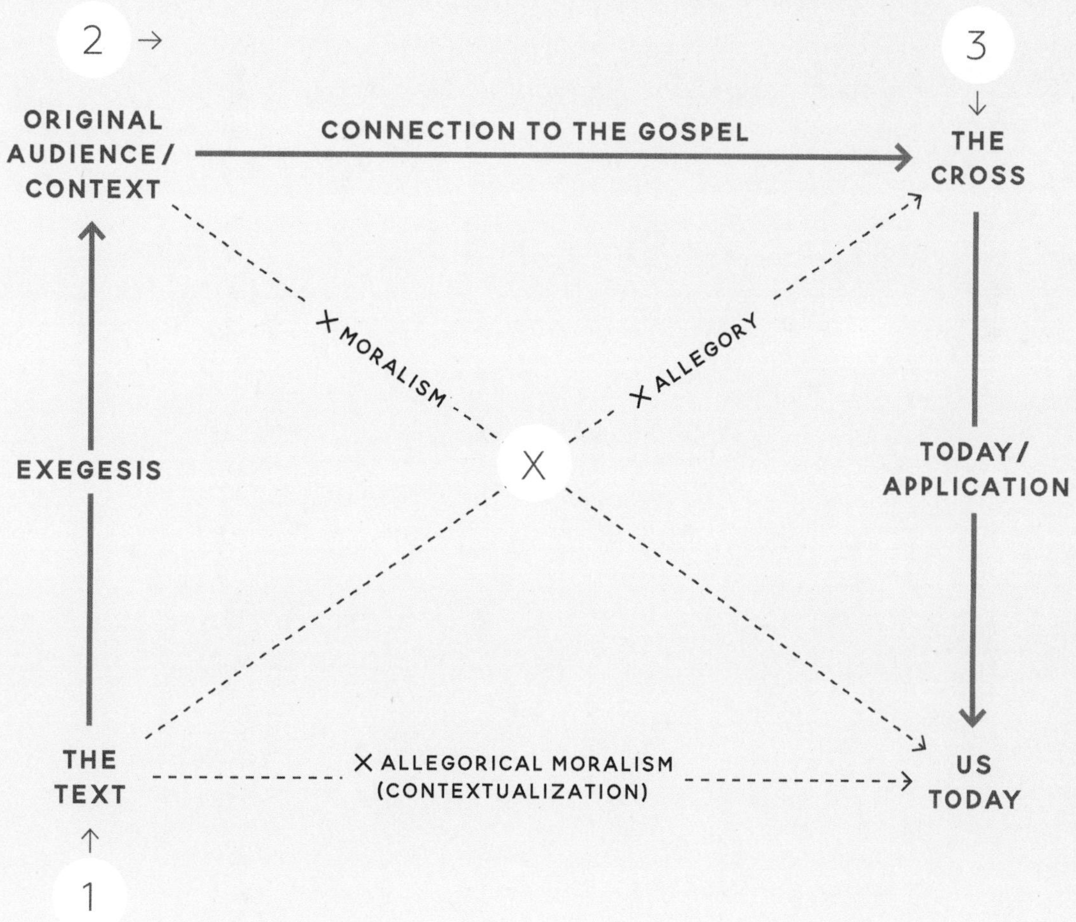

Graphic adapted from Edmund P. Clowney, *Preaching and Biblical Theology* (Grand Rapids: Eerdmans, 1961), 98-112.

There are many biblical theology themes that develop throughout Scripture. While this list is not exhaustive by any means, it includes many of the most prominent biblical theology themes.

Biblical Theology Themes

COVENANTS

KINGDOM

PRIESTHOOD

SACRIFICE

TABERNACLE & TEMPLE

FEASTS

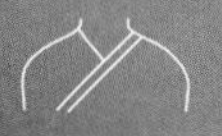
CLOTHING

CLEAN & UNCLEAN

WORSHIP

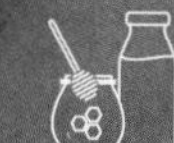
PROMISED LAND

IMMANUEL

EXODUS & EXILE

GARDEN & WILDERNESS

MARRIAGE

LIGHT & DARKNESS

OFFSPRING & SEED

BLESSING & CURSE

Study Reflection

Read: Psalm 19

The Word of the Lord is a great treasure, more valuable and desirable than the purest gold and sweeter to the soul than the sweetest honey. It gives wisdom and knowledge. It informs, and it transforms. The Word of God produces good and righteous things in the life of the believer, and we cannot overestimate its value to us. As you wrap up this study, we want to challenge you to take what you have learned and put it to use as you dive deeper into the Bible. Take these tools, and continue to practice using them, not only so that you can gain knowledge about God but so you can also know Him. When we seek the Lord and we come to know Him, the natural outpouring is that we will love Him and love others. To know the Lord, to love the Lord, and to love others is the calling on the life of every person, and we cannot do it apart from His Word.

Answer the following questions as you reflect over this study.

Why is studying Scripture important?

What is the most valuable thing you have learned in this study?

Are there any concepts that you learned for which you feel you need more practice in order to use them well? How will you intentionally work on those skills?

What has God revealed to you about Himself during this study?

How will you approach Bible study differently moving forward?

In light of all you have learned, write a prayer asking God to help you in your present and future Bible study endeavors.

PSALM 19:7

—

The instruction of the Lord is perfect, renewing one's life; the testimony of the Lord is trustworthy, making the inexperienced wise.

Biblical Symbolism

Symbol	Used in Scripture:	Scripture to reference:
BLOOD = LIFE	425 times	Hebrews 9:22, Genesis 9:4, Ephesians 1:7
BREAD = PROVISION	331 times	Proverbs 9:5, Isaiah 33:16, John 6:48
LIGHT = GOODNESS, TRUTH	259 times	Job 12:22, Psalm 27:1, John 12:46
SHEEP = FOLLOWERS	202 times	Psalm 100:3, Isaiah 53:6, John 10:11
LAMB = SPOTLESS SACRIFICE	198 times	John 1:29, 1 Corinthians 5:7, Exodus 12

Symbol	*Used in Scripture:*	*Scripture to reference:*
ROCK = FOUNDATION, SECURITY	146 times	Deuteronomy 32:4, Psalm 31:2, Matthew 16:18
SHEPHERD = LEADER, CARETAKER	117 times	Psalm 23:1, Isaiah 40:11, Revelation 7:17
TABERNACLE = GOD'S DWELLING PLACE	108 times	Exodus 25:8, Ezekiel 37:27, Revelation 21:3
WHITE = PURITY	62 times	Psalm 51:7, Matthew 28:3, Revelation 7:9
PURPLE = ROYAL	53 times	Exodus 39:1, Judges 8:26, Mark 15:17

Timeline of Scripture

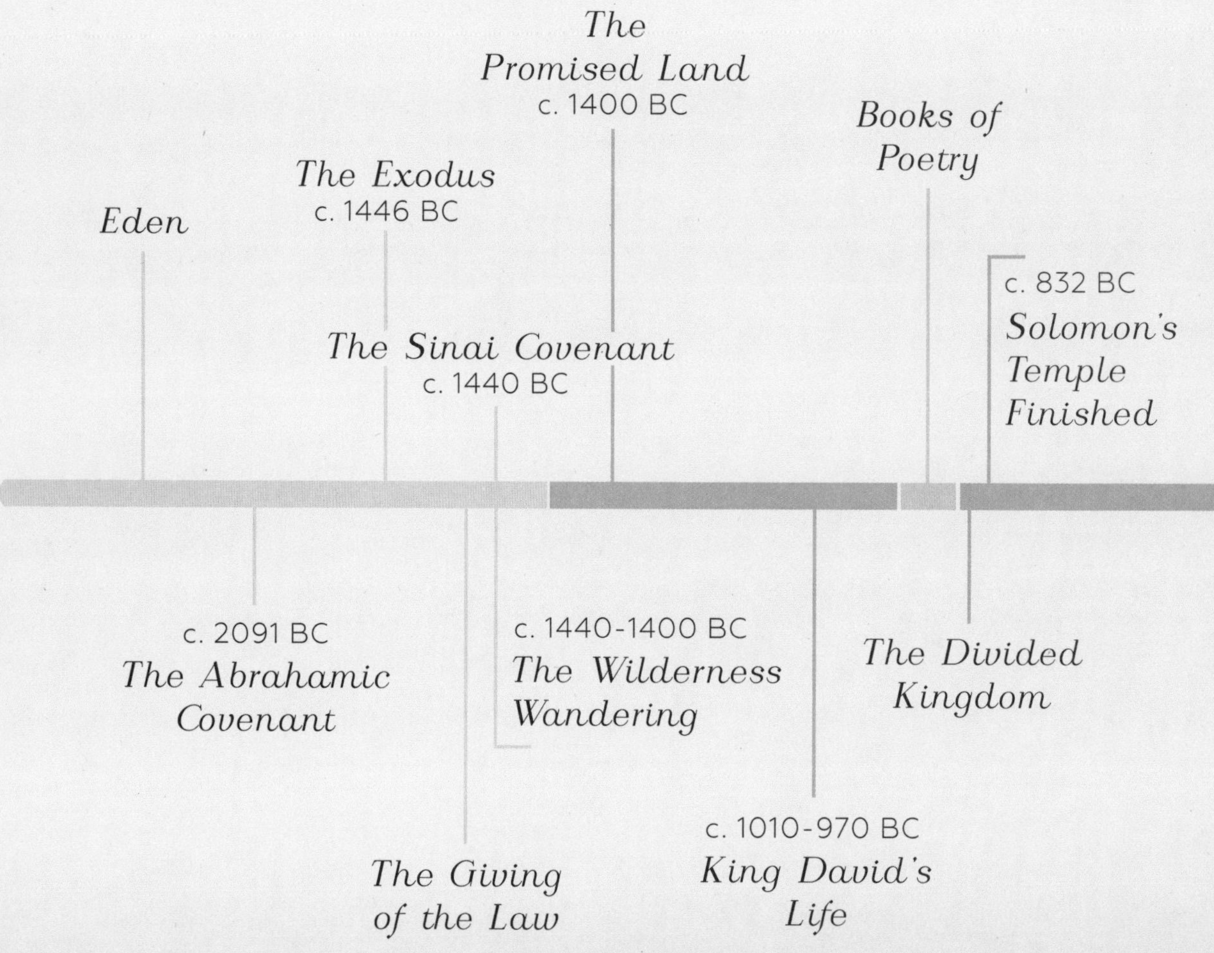

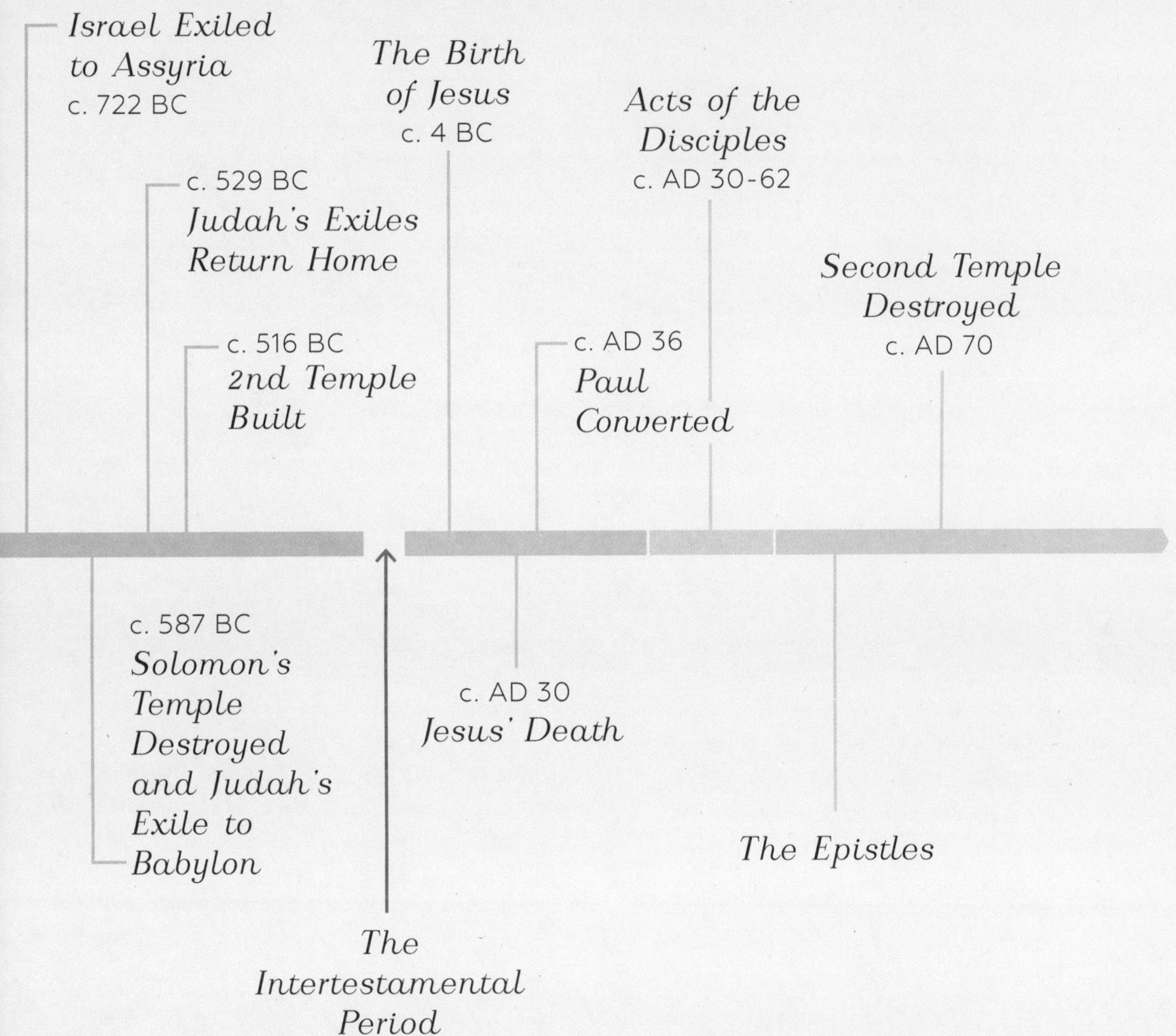
Israel Exiled to Assyria
c. 722 BC
c. 529 BC
Judah's Exiles Return Home
c. 516 BC
2nd Temple Built
The Birth of Jesus
c. 4 BC
Acts of the Disciples
c. AD 30-62
c. AD 36
Paul Converted
Second Temple Destroyed
c. AD 70
c. 587 BC
Solomon's Temple Destroyed and Judah's Exile to Babylon
The Intertestamental Period
c. AD 30
Jesus' Death
The Epistles

Christ in all of Scripture

All of Scripture points us to Jesus. We read the Old Testament to see Jesus. We read the New Testament to see Jesus. It is all about Jesus. Jesus Himself speaks to this truth. In Luke 24, He appears to the disciples and teaches them, "beginning with Moses and all the Prophets, he interpreted for them the things concerning himself in all the Scriptures." Jesus says similarly in John 5, "Moses wrote of me." We can find Jesus in every book of the Bible, but we must learn how to look for Him.

PROMISES & PROPHECY

Many parts of Scripture contain explicit messianic prophecies that predict the coming of Jesus Christ. Many promises and prophecies have an immediate and partial historical fulfillment but a complete fulfillment in Jesus Christ.

The prophecy of a suffering servant
Isaiah 53:5

Fulfillment found in the crucifixion of Christ
Matthew 26-28, Mark 14-15, Luke 22-23, John 18-19

NEED FOR CHRIST

Every problem, every bit of pain and suffering we experience, stems from the fall in Genesis 3, and the solution is Jesus Christ.

Sin enters the world causing separation between God and man
Genesis 3:8-24

Sin struggle within ourself
Romans 7:15-25

TYPOLOGY

A type of Christ is a person, an object, an institution, etc. that serves to point forward to the true substance. A type will have similarities and differences to Christ and will point forward to Him as the true and better fulfillment of the thing that partially images Him.

Sin enters the world through one man, Adam
Genesis 3

Life is given through one man, Jesus Christ: Jesus is the true and better Adam
Romans 5:12-21

Transition Words

There are many different types of transition words. These different transition words or phrases are useful because they show the relationship between different passages, and they provide a sense of cohesion in the author's writing. The meaning of the text is more fully, clearly, and accurately seen because of these transition words, so they are important to note.

USED TO SHOW:	EXAMPLES:
Emphasis	*importantly, absolutely, in particular, it should be noted, etc.*
Addition	*furthermore, also, to, along with, moreover, but also, etc.*
Contrast	*nevertheless, despite, in contrast to, while, where as, even so, etc.*
Order	*first or firstly, before, subsequently, above all, following, first and foremost, etc.*
Result	*therefore, thus, hence, for this reason, due to, etc.*
Illustration	*for example, such as, including, namely, like, etc.*
Comparison	*similarly, likewise, just as, in the same way, etc.*
Summary	*in conclusion, altogether, etc.*
Reason	*because of, with this in mind, in fact, in order to, due to, etc.*
Condition	*if, in case, unless, etc.*
Concession	*admittedly, even so, although, even though, however, etc.*

Bible Highlighting

Bible highlighting is a tool that can be helpful in facilitating deep, intentional Bible study. Bible highlighting helps us to slow down and take a closer look at the passage when our tendency is to read through it quickly and miss important details. There is no one right way to use Bible highlighting, but here are some examples of systems you can use. Feel free to use one of these or to create your own system

Yellow = Character of God

Blue = Redemption

Green = Commands to Obey

Orange = Nature of Man/Flesh + Sins to Avoid

Purple = Book-Specific Key Themes

Pink = Verses to Memorize

Yellow = Attributes of God

Orange = Attributes of Man

Blue = Prophecies of Christ, Types and Shadows of Christ, etc.

Green = Commands and Principles

Purple = Verses to Pray

Pink = Covenants, God's Promises to His People

Yellow = Things about God (His attributes, His promises)

Orange = Things about Man (our needs, struggles, sin issues)

Blue = Faith

Green = Adoration

Purple = Book Specific Themes

Pink = Commands

Yellow = Who wrote it?

Orange = To whom was it written?

Blue = Where is this taking place?

Green = When was this written?

Purple = Why was this written?

Green = When was this written?

Orange = To whom was it written?

Blue = Where is this taking place?

Yellow = Who wrote it?

Thank you for studying God's Word with us!

CONNECT WITH US

@thedailygraceco
@kristinschmucker

CONTACT US

info@thedailygraceco.com

SHARE

#thedailygraceco
#lampandlight

VISIT US ONLINE

thedailygraceco.com

MORE DAILY GRACE

The Daily Grace App
Daily Grace Podcast